FAA-S-8081-26A

U.S. Department
of Transportation

**Federal Aviation
Administration**

GENERAL

AVIATION MECHANIC GENERAL

Practical Test Standards

July 2012

FLIGHT STANDARDS SERVICE
Washington, DC 20591

AVIATION MECHANIC GENERAL

PRACTICAL TEST STANDARDS

2012

FLIGHT STANDARDS SERVICE
Washington, D.C. 20591

NOTE

FAA-S-8081-26A, Aviation Mechanic General Practical Test Standards (PTS) supersedes FAA-S-8081-26 dated June 2003.

This PTS will be effective November 1, 2012.

MAJOR ENHANCEMENTS

- Removed the core competency element requirements (objective 2) for each subject area.
- There are now only 2 objectives for each subject area:
    - Objective 1: Exhibits knowledge in, oral elements.
    - Objective 2: Demonstrates skill to perform practical elements.
- Added and/or revised elements within objective 2 to expand the selection of projects for the DME.
- Added new subject area "M" Human Factors/Maintenance Resource Management (MRM).
- Revised introduction to include International Civil Aviation Organization (ICAO) references to aircraft maintenance performance, eligibility, skill, knowledge, and experience requirements.
- Updated references to FAA orders, instructional materials, and inspector guidance.

FOREWORD

This Aviation Mechanic General Practical Test Standards book has been published by the Federal Aviation Administration (FAA) to establish the standards for the Aviation Mechanic General Practical Test. The passing of this practical test is a required step toward obtaining the Aviation Mechanic Certificate with Airframe and/or Powerplant ratings. **FAA inspectors and Designated Mechanic Examiners (DMEs) shall conduct practical tests in compliance with these standards.** Applicants should find these standards helpful in practical test preparation.

/s/ 7/18/2012
Raymond Towles, for

_____

John Allen, Director
Flight Standards Service

CONTENTS

SUBJECT AREAS

SECTION I—AVIATION MECHANIC GENERAL

Introduction

The Federal Aviation Administration (FAA) aircraft mechanic's oral and practical test(s) are outcome-based examinations. Before being issued any airframe and/or powerplant certificate, all applicants must demonstrate the minimum level of knowledge and skills for the rating sought.

Skill tests are significant as they measure the applicant's ability to logically think and objectively apply their knowledge, while demonstrating the physical skills that enable them to carry out aircraft maintenance in a professional and safe manner.

Satisfactory demonstration of each skill test is evidence the applicant meets the acceptable degree of competency for the certificate or rating sought.

This PTS is available for download, free of charge, at:

www.faa.gov

Comments regarding this PTS should be sent to:

AFS630comments@faa.gov

-OR-

U.S. Department of Transportation
Federal Aviation Administration
Regulatory Support Division
Airman Testing Standards Branch, AFS-630
P.O. Box 25082
Oklahoma City, OK 73125

Practical Test Standard Concept

Title 49 U.S. Code, Subpart III, Chapter 447 is the foundation for the FAA's safety regulations, and provides flexibility through FAA Order 8900.2, General Aviation Airman Designee Handbook, to examine and issue an airman certificate. This order is policy and mandatory standardized procedures for those who administer all aviation mechanic oral and practical tests.

NOTE: A designee conducting an oral and/or practical test must not test more than one applicant at a time, unless authorized in accordance with FAA Order 8900.1, Flight Standards Information Management System and FAA Order 8900.2.

Definitions within:

- **Competency**—a combination of skills, knowledge, and attitudes required to perform a task to the prescribed standard.
- **Knowledge**—(oral) elements are indicated by use of the words *"Exhibits knowledge in...."*
- **Skill**—(practical) elements are indicated by the use of the words *"Demonstrates the skill to perform...."*

This practical test book is a variety of technical projects or tasks containing subject areas included in the FAA written knowledge test as the current minimum required curriculum, which is prescribed in Title 14 of the Code of Federal Regulations (14 CFR) part 147 appendices.

Compliance with these procedures makes certain that airman applicants meet a satisfactory level of competency and workmanship required for certification.

Every applicant is required to demonstrate a minimum satisfactorily competency level, regardless of their previous education background.

Adherence to the following standards is mandatory when evaluating an applicant's test performance for an FAA Airframe and/or Powerplant Certificate:

- International Civil Aviation Organization (ICAO) Annex 1: 4.2.1.5
- 14 CFR part 65, section 65.79
- FAA Order 8900.2

All applicants for a FAA Aviation Mechanic Certificate must qualify by meeting the prescribed requirements as stated in 14 CFR part 65, section 65.77. They must additionally pass a written knowledge test, and the oral and practical tests for the certificate and/or rating sought, in accordance with the following standards:

- ICAO Annex 1: 4.2.1.3
- 14 CFR part 65, section 65.77

FAA written knowledge tests contain topics that include the construction and maintenance of aircraft, relevant FAA regulations, basic principles for installation and maintenance of propellers, and powerplants, depending on the certificate and rating sought, based on the following standards:

- ICAO Annex 1: 4.2.1.2
- 14 CFR part 65, section 65.75

Aviation maintenance instructors and applicants should find these standards helpful during training and preparing for the skill test, which are required under 14 CFR part 65, section 65.79.

Reference List:

14 CFR part 1	Definitions and Abbreviations
14 CFR part 3	General Requirements
14 CFR part 21	Certification Procedures for Products and Parts
14 CFR part 39	Airworthiness Directives
14 CFR part 43	Maintenance, Preventive Maintenance Rebuilding, and Alteration
14 CFR part 45	Identification and Registration Marking
14 CFR part 47	Aircraft Registration
14 CFR part 65	Certification: Airmen Other Than Flight Crewmembers
14 CFR part 91	Air Traffic and General Operating Rules
AC 20-62E	Eligibility, Quality, and Identification of Aeronautical Replacement Parts
AC 21-12B	Application for U.S. Airworthiness Certificate
AC 23-21	Airworthiness Compliance Checklist Used to Substantiate Major Alteration for Small Airplanes
AC 23.1309-1E	System Safety Analysis and Assessment for Part 23 Airplanes
AC 43.9C	Maintenance Records
AC 43.9-1F	Instructions for Completion of FAA Form 337
AC 43-206	Inspection, Prevention, Control and Repair or Corrosion on Avionics Equipment
AC 43-210	Standardized Procedures for Requesting Field Approval of Data, Major Alteration and Repairs
AC 43.13-1B	Acceptable Methods, Techniques and Practices A/C Inspection & Repair
AC 43.13-2B	Acceptable Methods, Techniques and Practices- Aircraft Alterations

FAA-H-8083-1	Aircraft Weight and Balance Handbook
FAA-H-8083-30	Aviation Maintenance Technician Handbook—General
FAA-H-8083-31	Aviation Maintenance Technician Handbook—Airframe
ICAO	International Civil Aviation Organization Annex 1, Personnel Licensing

Each subject area has an objective. The objective lists the important knowledge and skill elements that must be utilized by the examiner in planning and administering aviation mechanic tests, and that applicants must be prepared to satisfactorily perform.

EXAMINER is used in this standard to denote either the FAA Inspector or FAA Designated Mechanic Examiner (DME) who conducts the practical test.

Use of the Practical Test Standards

The FAA requires that all practical tests be conducted in accordance with the appropriate Aviation Mechanic Practical Test Standards and the policies and standardized procedures set forth in the current revision of FAA Order 8900.2, General Aviation Airman Designee Handbook.

When using this PTS, the examiner must evaluate the applicant's knowledge and skill in sufficient depth to determine that the objective for each subject area element selected is met. If the element selected in one subject area has already been evaluated in another area, they need not be repeated. For example, the applicant need not be evaluated in SUBJECT AREA H. MATHEMATICS, ELEMENT **H10**. Add, subtract, multiply, and divide positive and negative numbers. (Level 3). If that ELEMENT was sufficiently observed during the completion of "SUBJECT AREA C. WEIGHT AND BALANCE, ELEMENT **C4**. Compute forward and aft loaded c.g.(Level 3).

An applicant is not permitted to know before testing begins which selections in each subject area are to be included in his/her test. Therefore, an applicant should be well prepared in **all** oral and skill areas included in the practical test standard.

Further information and requirements for conducting a practical test is contained in FAA Order 8900.2.

Aviation Mechanic Practical Test Prerequisites

All applicants must have met the prescribed experience requirements as stated in 14 CFR part 65, section 65.77 or be an authorized school student per 14 CFR part 65, section 65.80. (See FAA Order 8900.2 for information about testing under the provisions of 14 CFR part 65, section 65.80.)

Examiner Responsibility

All applicants must demonstrate an approval for return to service standard, where applicable and demonstrate the ability to locate and apply the required reference materials, where applicable. In instances where an approval for return to service standard cannot be achieved, the applicant must be able to explain why the return to service standard was not met (e.g., when tolerances are outside of a product's limitations).

The examiner must personally observe all practical projects performed by the applicant. The examiner who conducts the practical test is responsible for determining that the applicant meets acceptable standards of knowledge and skill in the assigned subject areas within the appropriate practical test standard. Since there is no formal division between the knowledge and skill portions of the practical test, this becomes an ongoing process throughout the test.

The following terms may be reviewed with the applicant prior to, or during, element assignment.

1. **Inspect**—means to examine by sight and/or touch (with or without inspection enhancing tools/equipment).
2. **Check**—means to verify proper operation.
3. **Troubleshoot**—means to analyze and identify malfunctions.
4. **Service**—means to perform functions that assure continued operation.
5. **Repair**—means to correct a defective condition. Repair of an airframe or powerplant system includes component replacement and adjustment, but not component repair.
6. **Overhaul**—means disassembled, cleaned inspected, repaired as necessary, and reassembled.

Performance Levels

The following is a detailed description of the meaning of each level.

Level 1

- Know basic facts and principles.
- Be able to find information, and follow directions and written instructions.
- Locate methods, procedures, instructions, and reference material.
- Interpretation of information not required.
- No skill demonstration is required.

Example:

Z3b. Locate specified nondestructive testing methods. (Level 1)

Performance Standard: The applicant will locate information for nondestructive testing.

Level 2

- Know and understand principles, theories, and concepts.
- Be able to find and interpret maintenance data and information, and perform basic operations using the appropriate data, tools, and equipment.
- A high level of skill is not required.

Example:

Z3c. Detect electrical leakage in electrical connections, terminal strips, and cable harness (at least ten will have leakage faults). (Level 2)

Performance Standard: Using appropriate maintenance data and a multimeter, the applicant will identify items with leakage faults.

Level 3 (This is the approval for return to service standards).

- Know, understand, and apply facts, principles, theories, and concepts.
- Understand how they relate to the total operation and maintenance of aircraft.
- Be able to make independent and accurate airworthiness judgments.
- Perform all skill operations to a return-to-service standard using appropriate data, tools, and equipment. Inspections are performed in accordance with acceptable or approved data.
- A fairly high skill level is required.

Example:

Z3e. Check control surface travel. (Level 3)

Performance Standard: Using type certificate data sheets and the manufacturer's service manual, the applicant will measure the control surface travel, compare the travel to the maintenance data, and determine if the travel is within limits.

Satisfactory Performance

The practical test is passed if the applicant demonstrates the prescribed proficiency in the assigned elements in each subject area to the required standard. Applicants shall not be expected to memorize all mathematical formulas that may be required in the performance of various elements in this practical test standard. However, where relevant, applicants must be able to locate and apply necessary formulas to obtain correct solutions.

Unsatisfactory Performance

If the applicant does not meet the standards of any of the elements performed (knowledge or skill elements), the associated subject area is failed, and thus the practical test is failed. The examiner or the applicant may discontinue testing any time after the failure of a subject area. In any case, the applicant is entitled to credit for only those subject areas satisfactorily completed. See the current revision of FAA Order 8900.2 for further information about retesting and allowable credit for subject areas satisfactorily completed.

Typical areas of unsatisfactory performance and grounds for disqualification include the following.

1. Any action or lack of action by the applicant that requires corrective intervention by the examiner for reasons of safety.
2. Failure to follow acceptable or approved maintenance procedures while performing skill (practical) projects.
3. Exceeding tolerances stated in the maintenance instructions.
4. Failure to recognize improper procedures.
5. The inability to perform to a return to service standard, where applicable.
6. Inadequate knowledge in any of the subject areas.

SECTION I—AVIATION MECHANIC GENERAL

A. BASIC ELECTRICITY

REFERENCE: FAA-H-8083-30.

Objective.   To determine that the applicant:

1. Exhibits knowledge in, as a minimum, two of the following elements—

    a. sources and/or effects of capacitance in a circuit.
    b. uses of capacitance in a circuit.
    c. sources and/or effects of inductance in a circuit.
    d. uses of inductance in a circuit.
    e. operation of basic AC and/or DC electrical circuits.
    f. Ohm's law.
    g. Kirchhoff's law(s).
    h. procedures used in the measurement of voltage, current, and/or resistance.
    i. determining power used in simple circuits.
    j. troubleshooting, and/or repair or alteration using electrical circuit diagrams.
    k. common types of defects that may occur in an installed battery system.
    l. aircraft battery theory/operation.
    m. servicing aircraft batteries.

2. Demonstrates skill to perform, as a minimum, one of the following elements—

    A1.   Install wires in an electrical connector plug. (Level 3)
    A2.   Measure voltage, resistance, current, or continuity in a circuit and determine the appropriateness of the measurement. (Level 3)
    A3.   Calculate and measure aircraft electrical power requirements. (Level 2)
    A4.   Calculate and measure total capacitance in an electrical circuit (Level 2)
    A5.   Read and interpret aircraft electrical circuit diagrams, including solid state devices and logic functions. (Level 3)
    A6.   Determine or measure for open electrical circuits. (Level 3)
    A7.   Interpret electrical system shorts. (Level 2)
    A8.   Measure electrical system voltages. (Level 3)
    A9.   Measure electrical system component resistance. (Level 3)
    A10.   Compute voltage of electrical circuits. (Level 3)
    A11.   Measure resistance, current, and/or voltage in an electrical circuit. (Level 3)

A12. Calculate and measure total inductance in an electrical circuit. (Level 2)

A13. Identify commonly used aircraft electrical symbols. (Level 2)

A14. Interpret aircraft electrical circuit diagrams. (Level 2)

A15. Service an aircraft battery. (Level 3)

A16. Inspect an aircraft battery. (Level 3)

A17. Remove and install an aircraft battery. (Level 3)

A18. Inspect battery compartments. (Level 3)

A19. Measure the voltage drop across a resistor. (Level 3)

B. AIRCRAFT DRAWINGS

REFERENCE: FAA-H-8083-30.

Objective.   To determine that the applicant:

1.   Exhibits knowledge in, as a minimum, two of the following elements—

    a.   characteristics and/or uses of any of the various types of drawings/blueprints and/or system schematics.
    b.   the meaning of any of the lines and symbols commonly used in aircraft sketches/drawings/blueprints.
    c.   using charts or graphs.
    d.   troubleshooting an aircraft system or component(s) using drawings/blueprints and/or system schematics.
    e.   inspection of an aircraft system or component(s) using drawings/blueprints and/or system schematics.
    f.   repair or alteration of an aircraft system or component(s) using drawings/blueprints and/or schematics.
    g.   use of drawings/blueprints in component fabrication.
    h.   terms used in conjunction with aircraft drawings/blueprints and/or system schematics.

2.   Demonstrates skill to perform, as a minimum, one of the following elements—

    B1.   Identify lines and symbols. (Level 2)
    B2.   Interpret dimensions. (Level 2)
    B3.   Use installation diagrams and/or schematics. (Level 3)
    B4.   Draw a sketch of a major repair or alteration. (Level 3)
    B5.   Use blueprint information. (Level 3)
    B6.   Use graphs and charts. (Level 3)
    B7.   Identify blueprint changes. (Level 2)
    B8.   Determine material requirements from a drawing. (Level 2)

FAA-S-8081-26A

C. WEIGHT AND BALANCE

REFERENCE: FAA-H-8083-30.

Objective.   To determine that the applicant:

1.   Exhibits knowledge in, as a minimum, two of the following elements—

    a.   the purpose(s) of weighing or reweighing.
    b.   general preparations for weighing, with emphasis on aircraft preparation and/or weighing area considerations.
    c.   the general location of airplane center of gravity (CG) in relation to the center of lift for most fixed main airfoils.
    d.   definitions of any of the following: datum, arm, moment (positive or negative), or moment index.
    e.   the meaning and/or application of any terms/nomenclature associated with weight and balance other than those mentioned in element "d" above, including but not limited to any of the following: tare, ballast, and residual fuel/oil.
    f.   procedures for finding any of the following: datum, arm, moment (positive or negative), or moment index.
    g.   purpose and/or application of mean aerodynamic chord (MAC).
    h.   adverse loading considerations.

2.   Demonstrates skill to perform, as a minimum, one of the following elements—

    C1.   Compute the empty weight and empty weight CG of an aircraft. (Level 3)
    C2.   Check aircraft weighing scales for calibration. (Level 2)
    C3.   Establish new weight and balance data for an aircraft after an equipment change. (Level 3)
    C4.   Compute forward and aft loaded CG. (Level 3)
    C5.   Prepare an aircraft for weighing. (Level 2)
    C6.   Determine a location for permanent ballast to bring an aircraft back into balance. (Level 2)
    C7.   Make a maintenance record entry for a weight and balance change. (Level 3)
    C8.   Compute the amount of fuel needed for minimum fuel for weight and balance computations. (Level 3)
    C9.   Weigh an aircraft. (Level 3)
    C10.   Record scale readings from a weighed aircraft. (Level 2)
    C11.   Compute weight and balance CG. for a helicopter. (Level 3)
    C12.   Calculate the moment of an item of equipment. (Level 3)
    C13.   Determine the distance between the forward and aft CG limits of a helicopter. (Level 3)

C14. Identify tare items. (Level 3)

C15. Locate weight and balance information. (Level 1)

C16. Locate datum. (Level 1)

C17. Locate the baggage compartment placarding requirements for an aircraft. (Level 1)

C18. Revise an aircraft equipment list after equipment change. (Level 3)

C19. Determine the weight and location of required ballast. (Level 2)

C20. Calculate the change needed to correct an overweight or out of balance condition. (Level 3)

D. FLUID LINES AND FITTINGS

REFERENCE: FAA-H-8083-30.

Objective. To determine that the applicant:

1. Exhibits knowledge in, as a minimum, two of the following elements—

    a. tubing materials.
    b. tubing materials application.
    c. tubing sizes.
    d. flexible hose material.
    e. flexible hose materials application.
    f. flexible hose sizes.
    g. flexible hose identification.
    h. AN, MS, and/or AC plumbing fittings.
    i. rigid line fabrication techniques/practices.
    j. rigid line installation techniques/practices.
    k. flexible hose fabrication techniques/practices.
    l. flexible hose installation techniques/practices.

2. Demonstrates skill to perform, as a minimum, one of the following elements—

    D1. Make a replacement fluid line (aluminum or stainless steel).
    (Level 3)
    D2. Form a bead on tubing. (Level 3)
    D3. Fabricate a flare on tubing. (Level 3)
    D4. Fabricate and install fittings on a flexible hose. (Level 3)
    D5. Identify defects in metal tubing. (Level 2)
    D6. Repair a section of tubing. (Level 3)
    D7. Install and secure a fluid line with clamps. (Level 3)
    D8. Identify fluid and air lines that may be installed on aircraft.
    (Level 2)
    D9. Identify different flexible fluid lines. (Level 2)
    D10. Determine fluid line routing. (Level 3)
    D11. Fabricate and install metal tubing. (Level 3)
    D12. Identify aircraft fittings. (Level 2)
    D13. Install a flareless-fitting-tube connection. (Level 3)

E. MATERIALS AND PROCESSES

REFERENCE: FAA-H-8083-30.

Objective.   To determine that the applicant:

1. Exhibits knowledge in, as a minimum, two of the following elements—

    a.   any of the metals commonly used in aircraft and their general application.

    b.   composites and other nonmetallic components and their general application.

    c.   heat-treated parts precautions, using DD or "icebox" rivets.

    d.   typical wood materials and fabric coverings.

    e.   visible characteristics of acceptable and/or unacceptable welds.

    f.   precision measurement and precision measurement tools.

    g.   using inspection techniques/methods, including any of the following: visual, metallic ring test, dye/fluorescent penetrant, magnetic particle, and/or eddy current.

    h.   identification, selection, installation, and/or use of aircraft hardware.

    i.   safe tying of components and/or hardware.

    j.   finding information about material types for specific application(s).

2. Demonstrates skill to perform, as a minimum, one of the following elements—

    E1.   Perform a visual inspection of various welds. (Level 2)

    E2.   Perform magnetic particle inspection of a steel part. (Level 2)

    E3.   Identify different kinds of aircraft materials and hardware by using manufacturer's markings. (Level 2)

    E4.   Select and install aircraft bolts. (Level 3)

    E5.   Perform dye penetrant inspection of an aircraft part. (Level 2)

    E6.   Make precision measurements with an instrument that has a vernier micrometer scale. (Level 3)

    E7.   Check the alignment of a shaft. (Level 3)

    E8.   Safety wires a turnbuckle, using an approved method. (Level 3)

    E9.   Identify aircraft control cable. (Level 3)

    E10.   Fabricate a cable assembly using a swaged end fitting. (Level 3)

    E11.   Select the correct aluminum alloy for a structural repair. (Level 2)

    E12.   Identify rivets by physical characteristics. (Level 2)

    E13.   Determine suitability of materials for aircraft repairs. (Level 2)

    E14.   Determine if certain materials ca be welded. (Level 2)

    E15.   Distinguish between heat-treated and non-heat-treated aluminum alloys. (Level 2)

    E16.   Determine required torque value of given item. (Level 3)

    E17.   Check for proper calibration of a micrometer. (Level 2)

    E18.   Identify proper installation procedures for a seal, backup ring, and/or gasket. (Level 2)

F. GROUND OPERATION AND SERVICING

REFERENCE: FAA-H-8083-30.

Objective. To determine that the applicant:

1. Exhibits knowledge in, as a minimum, two of the following elements—

   a. general procedures for towing aircraft.
   b. Air Traffic Control (ATC) considerations/requirements for towing aircraft on or across active runways.
   c. general procedures for starting, ground operating, and/or taxiing a reciprocating engine powered aircraft.
   d. general procedures for starting, ground operating, and/or taxiing a turbine engine powered aircraft.
   e. the hazards associated with starting, ground operating, and/or taxiing aircraft and procedures for preventing, minimizing or otherwise managing any of them.
   f. procedures for refueling and/or defueling aircraft.
   g. oxygen system safety practices/precautions.
   h. characteristics of aviation gasoline and/or turbine fuels, including basic types and means of identification.
   i. fuel contamination hazards.
   j. fuel additives commonly used in the field.
   k. use of automobile fuel in aircraft engines.
   l. types/classes of fires, using proper fire extinguishers/methods.

2. Demonstrates skill to perform, as a minimum, one of the following elements—

   F1. Start and operate an aircraft reciprocating engine. (Level 2)
   F2. Start and operate an aircraft turbine engine. (Level 2)
   F3. Prepare an aircraft for engine starting. (Level 2)
   F4. Tie down and secure an aircraft for outside storage. (Level 2)
   F5. Connect a towbar to an aircraft and prepare for towing. (Level 2)
   F6. Use appropriate hand signals for the movement of aircraft. (Level 2)
   F7. Show the procedure for clearing a liquid lock in a reciprocating engine. (Level 2)
   F8. Fuel an aircraft (may be simulated). (Level 2)
   F9. Determine the remaining amount of fuel in an aircraft. (Level 2)
   F10. Select an approved fuel for an aircraft. (Level 2)
   F11. Inspect an aircraft fuel system for water contamination.(Level 2)
   F12. List the procedures for extinguishing fires in an engine induction system during starting. (Level 2)
   F13. Connect an external auxiliary power unit. (Level 2)
   F14. Identify different grades of aviation gasoline. (Level 2)
   F15 Secure a helicopter for high-wind conditions. (Level 2)
   F16. Secure a turbine-powered aircraft after engine shutdown. (Level 2)

G. CLEANING AND CORROSION CONTROL

REFERENCE: FAA-H-8083-30.

Objective. To determine that the applicant:

1. Exhibits knowledge in, as a minimum, two of the following elements—

   a. aircraft preparation for washing, and general aircraft cleaning (washing) procedures.
   b. post cleaning (washing) procedures.
   c. corrosion theory.
   d. types/effects of corrosion.
   e. conditions that cause corrosion.
   f. corrosion prone areas in aircraft.
   g. corrosion preventive maintenance procedures.
   h. inspection for and identification of corrosion in any of its various forms.
   i. corrosion removal and treatment procedures.
   j. use of Material Safety Data Sheets (MSDS).

2. Demonstrates skill to perform, as a minimum, one of the following elements—

   G1. Clean aluminum and/or magnesium parts with caustic cleaners. (Level 3)
   G2. Identify approved cleaning agents. (Level 2)
   G3. Clean assigned area of aircraft. (Level 3)
   G4. Identify different types of corrosion. (Level 2)
   G5. Remove corrosion from an aluminum alloy. (Level 3)
   G6. Apply protective coating to a metallic material. (Level 3)
   G7. Remove iron oxide. (Level 3)
   G8. Remove grease or oil from an appropriate part or component. (Level 3)
   G9. Mechanically remove paint from a corroded aircraft part and determine extent of corrosion. (Level 3)
   G10. Locate procedures for preparing aircraft parts for extended storage. (Level 1)
   G11. Clean and protect plastics and/or composite materials. (Level 3)
   G12. Apply a protective coating to a metal surface. (Level 3)

H. MATHEMATICS

REFERENCE: FAA-H-8083-30.

Objective.   To determine that the applicant:

1.   Exhibits knowledge in, as a minimum, two of the following elements—

   a.   areas of various geometrical shapes.
   b.   volumes of various geometrical shapes.
   c.   definitions/descriptions of geometrical terms, including but not limited to any of the following: polygon, pi, diameter, radius, and hypotenuse.
   d.   ratio problems, including examples of where or how they may be used in relation to aircraft maintenance or system(s) operation.
   e.   proportion problems, including examples of where or how they may be used in relation to aircraft maintenance or system(s) operation.
   f.   percentage problems, including examples of where or how they may be used in relation to aircraft maintenance or system(s) operation.
   g.   algebraic operations, including examples of where or how they may be used in relation to aircraft maintenance.
   h.   conditions or areas where metric conversion may be necessary.

2.   Demonstrates skill to perform, as a minimum, one of the following elements—

   H1.   Determine the square root of given numbers. (Level 2)
   H2.   Locate the instructions for determining square root. (Level 1)
   H3.   Locate formulas to determine area and/or volume. (Level 1)
   H4.   Compute the volume of a cylinder. (Level 3)
   H5.   Compute the area of a wing. (Level 3)
   H6.   Calculate the volume of a baggage compartment. (Level 3)
   H7.   Convert fractional numbers to decimal equivalents. (Level 3)
   H8.   Compare two numerical values using ratios. (Level 3)
   H9.   Compute compression ratio. (Level 3)
   H10.   Add, subtract, multiply, and/or divide positive and negative numbers. (Level 3)
   H11.   Compute the least common denominator of two or more fractions. (Level 3)
   H12.   Compute the torque value change when using a torque wrench with an extension. (Level 3)

NOTE: The practical portion of the Mathematics subject area may be tested simultaneously when performing calculation(s) in subject areas Basic Electricity and/or Weight and Balance.

I. MAINTENANCE FORMS AND RECORDS

REFERENCE: FAA-H-8083-30.

Objective. To determine that the applicant:

1. Exhibits knowledge in, as a minimum, two of the following elements—

    a. writing descriptions of work performed and approval for return to service after minor repairs or minor alterations.
    b. the content, form, and disposition of aircraft maintenance records reflecting approval for return to service after a 100-hour inspection.
    c. the content, form, and disposition of aircraft maintenance records reflecting disapproval for return to service after a 100-hour inspection.
    d. the recording content, form, and disposition requirements for certificated aviation mechanics (without an Inspection Authorization) that perform major repairs and/or major alterations.
    e. the inoperative instruments or equipment provisions of 14 CFR part 91.
    f. the definition/explanation of any of the terms used in relation to aircraft maintenance, such as overhaul(ed), rebuilt, time in service, maintenance, preventive maintenance, inspection, major alteration, major repair, minor alteration, and minor repair.

2. Demonstrates skill to perform, as a minimum, one of the following elements—

    I1.   Inspect an aircraft and prepare a condition report. (Level 3)
    I2.   Make a log book entry for a repair or alteration. (Level 3)
    I3.   Write a 100-hour inspection aircraft record entry. (Level 3)
    I4.   Write an AD compliance aircraft record entry. (Level 3)
    I5.   Complete an FAA Form 337. (Level 3)
    I6.   Determine aircraft airworthiness by examining maintenance record entries. (Level 3)
    I7.   Examine a FAA Form 337 for potential errors. (Level 3)
    I8.   Prepare a master AD list for a specific airframe, engine and/or propeller and determine applicability by make, model, and serial number. (Level 3)
    I9.   Write an annual inspection aircraft record entry. (Level 3)
    I10. Make a maintenance record entry for a propeller minor repair that was performed by an individual that is being supervised by an appropriately rated mechanic that will be approving the repair for return to service. (Level 3)

I11. Write a 100-hour inspection aircraft maintenance record entry for an aircraft not approved for return to service. (Level 3)

I12. Write a maintenance record entry for compliance with manufacturer's Service Bulletin, Service Instruction, or Service Letter. (Level 3)

I13. Create a current equipment list for an aircraft, listing all equipment installed. (Level 3)

I14. Make the required maintenance record entries for approval for return to service after a major repair or major alteration. (Level 3)

I15. Complete the proper part or component tag for a part of known condition. (Level 3)

I16. Make a maintenance record entry for the installation of a serviceable part. (Level 3)

I17. Prepare a list of discrepancies and unairworthy items following a 100-hour inspection. (Level 3)

J. BASIC PHYSICS

REFERENCE: FAA-H-8083-30.

Objective. To determine that the applicant:

1. Exhibits knowledge in, as a minimum, two of the following elements—

   a. any of the simple machines, how they function, and/or how mechanical advantage is applied in one or more specific examples.
   b. sound resonance, how it can be a hazard to aircraft, and how sound may be used to aid in inspecting aircraft.
   c. the relationship between fluid density and specific gravity.
   d. the characteristic of specific gravity of fluids and how it may be applied to aircraft maintenance.
   e. the general effects of pressure and temperature on gases and liquids and how the qualities of compressibility and/or incompressibility of gases and liquids are generally applied to aircraft systems.
   f. density altitude and the effects of temperature, and/or pressure, and/or humidity on aircraft and/or engine performance.
   g. heat, how it is manifested in matter, and how heat transfer is accomplished through conduction, and/or convection, and/or radiation.
   h. coefficient of linear (thermal) expansion as related to aircraft materials.
   i. aircraft structures and theory of flight/physics of lift.
   j. the operation of aerodynamic factors in the flight of airplanes and/or helicopters.
   k. the relationship between force, area, and pressure.
   l. the five forces or stresses affecting aircraft structures.
   m. the two forms of energy and how they apply to aircraft and/or aircraft systems.

2. Demonstrates skill to perform, as a minimum, one of the following elements—

   J1. Convert temperature from one scale to another, for example F° to C° or from C° to F°. (Level 2)

   J2. Determine density altitude. (Level 2)

   J3. Determine pressure altitude. (Level 2)

   J4. Calculate force, area, or pressure in a specific application. (Level 3)

   J5. Demonstrate the mechanical advantage of various types of levers. (Level 3)

   J6. Design an inclined plane on paper, indicating the mechanical advantage. (Level 2)

   J7. Identify changes in pressure and velocity as a fluid passes through a venturi. (Level 2)

   J8. Design a mechanical pulley system. (Level 2)

   J9. Determine density of a solid object with a specific gravity of less than one. (Level 2)

   J10. Determine horsepower for a given weight, distance, and time. (Level 2)

   J11. Calculate expansion due to temperature change. (Level 3)

K. MAINTENANCE PUBLICATIONS

REFERENCE: FAA-H-8083-30.

Objective. To determine that the applicant:

1. Exhibits knowledge in, as a minimum, two of the following elements—

    a. how a mechanic makes use of Type Certificate Data Sheets (TCDS) and/or Aircraft Specifications in conducting maintenance or inspections.
    b. aircraft maintenance manuals and associated publications including any of the following types of publications and how they are used: service bulletin, maintenance manual, overhaul manual, structural repair manual, or instructions   for continued airworthiness.
    c. the requirements of 14 CFR parts 43.13, 43.15, or 43.16 in the performance of maintenance.
    d. Airworthiness Directives (AD), including purpose and/or AD categories and/or ADs issued to other than aircraft.
    e. in what form individuals may receive FAA published AD summaries and/or how they may be obtained.
    f. the AD identification numbering system.
    g. FAA Advisory Circulars (ACs) including any of the following: significance of the AC numbering system, one or more examples of ACs issued to provide information in designated subject areas, and one or more examples of ACs issued to show a method acceptable to the FAA complying with the CFRs.
    h. the intent or function of the Aviation Maintenance Alerts.
    i. the Air Transport Association (ATA) Specification 100.

2. Demonstrates skill to perform, as a minimum, one of the following elements—

K1. Locate applicable FAA aircraft specifications and/or FAA type certificate data sheet for assigned aircraft or component. (Level 1)

K2. Locate the CG range of assigned aircraft using aircraft specifications and type certificate data sheets. (Level 1)

K3. Locate aircraft flight control travel limits. (Level 1)

K4. Locate manufacturer's service instructions. (Level 1)

K5. Determine applicability of an AD. (Level 3)

K6. Inspect aircraft for compliance with applicable ADs. (Level 3)

K7. Check a technical standard order (TSO) part for the proper TSO marking. (Level 3)

K8. Use a manufacturer's illustrated parts catalog to locate a specific part number. (Level 3)

K9. Locate supplemental type certificates (STCs) applicable to a specific aircraft. (Level 2)

K10. Determine the conformity of aircraft instrument range markings and/or placarding. (Level 3)

K11. Determine approved tires for installation on a given aircraft. (Level 3)

K12. Determine the ATA code for a specific item. (Level 3)

K13. Determine maximum allowable weight of a specific aircraft. (Level 3)

L. AVIATION MECHANIC PRIVILEGES AND LIMITATIONS

REFERENCES: 14 CFR part 65; AC 65-30A; FAA-H-8083-30.

Objective: To determine that the applicant:

1. Exhibits knowledge in, as a minimum, two of the following elements—

   a. required evidence of eligibility experience satisfactory to the Administrator.
   b. length of experience required for eligibility.
   c. practical experience required for eligibility.
   d. the privileges of a mechanic in relation to 100-hour and annual inspections.
   e. change of address reporting requirements.
   f. minimum age requirements.
   g. recent experience requirements to exercise privileges of a certificate.
   h. who is authorized to perform maintenance/inspection, preventive maintenance, rebuilding, or alteration and/or approve for return to service afterwards.
   i. causes for revocation or suspension.
   j. criteria for determining major and minor repair or alteration.

2. Demonstrates skill to perform, as a minimum, one of the following elements—

   L1. Determine if a given repair is major or minor. (Level 3)
   L2. Determine if a given alteration is major or minor. (Level 3)
   L3. Locate address change notification procedures. (Level 1)
   L4. List airframe mechanic privileges and limitations. (Level 2)
   L5. List powerplant mechanic privileges and limitations. (Level 2)
   L6. Locate mechanic privileges and limitations. (Level 1)
   L7. List the authorities to which an A&P mechanic must show his/her A&P certificate on demand. (Level 2)
   L8. Locate the 14 CFR reference that gives the privileges that a certified mechanic airframe or powerplant have. (Level 1)
   L9. List types of inspections that a certificated mechanic with airframe and powerplant ratings may perform and the 14 CFR reference for each one. (Level 2)
   L10. Determine references used in performing "preventive maintenance". (Level 2)
   L11. List the maintenance functions that a certificated mechanic may NOT supervise. (Level 2)

M. Human Factors/Maintenance Resource Management (MRM)

REFERENCES: 14 CFR part 65; AC 65-30A; FAA-H-8083-30.

Objective: To determine that the applicant:

1. Exhibits knowledge in, as a minimum, two of the following elements—

   a. safety management system (SMS) and/or MRM.
   b. human factors elements.
   c. positive aspects of human factors.
   d. evolution of maintenance human factors.
   e. types of human factors errors.
   f. twelve human factors for aircraft maintenance proficiency.

NOTE: The practical portion of the subject areas may be tested simultaneously with other subject areas provided all areas and testing levels are covered. For example, "Mathematics" can be combined when performing calculation(s) in subject areas such as Basic Electricity and/or Weight and Balance.

U.S. Department
of Transportation

**Federal Aviation
Administration**

FAA-S-8081-27A

AVIATION MECHANIC
AIRFRAME

Practical Test Standards

July 2012

FLIGHT STANDARDS SERVICE
Washington, DC 20591

AVIATION MECHANIC AIRFRAME

PRACTICAL TEST STANDARDS

2012

FLIGHT STANDARDS SERVICE
Washington, D.C. 20591

NOTE

FAA-S-8081-27A, Aviation Mechanic Airframe Practical Test Standards (PTS) supersedes FAA-S-8081-27 dated June 2003.

This PTS will be effective November 1, 2012.

MAJOR ENHANCEMENTS

- Removed the core competency element requirements (objective 2) for each subject area.
- There are now only 2 objectives for each subject area:
  - Objective 1: Exhibits knowledge in oral elements.
  - Objective 2: Demonstrates skill to perform, practical elements.
- Added and/or revised elements within objective 2 to expand the selection of projects for the DME.
- Added new subject area "M" Human Factors/Maintenance Resource Management (MRM).
- Revised introduction to include International Civil Aviation Organization (ICAO) references to aircraft maintenance performance, eligibility, skill, knowledge, and experience requirements.
- Updated references to FAA orders, instructional materials, and inspector guidance.

FOREWORD

This Aviation Mechanic Airframe Practical Test Standards book has been published by the Federal Aviation Administration (FAA) to establish the standards for the Aviation Mechanic Airframe Practical Test. The passing of this practical test is a required step toward obtaining the Aviation Mechanic certificate with an Airframe rating. **FAA inspectors and Designated Mechanic Examiners (DMEs) shall conduct practical tests in compliance with these standards.** Applicants should find these standards helpful in practical test preparation.

/s/ 7/18/2012
Raymond Towles, for

_____

John Allen, Director
Flight Standards Service

CONTENTS

SUBJECT AREAS

SECTION II—AIRFRAME STRUCTURES

SECTION III—AIRFRAME SYSTEMS AND COMPONENTS

INTRODUCTION

The Federal Aviation Administration (FAA) aircraft mechanic's oral and practical test(s) are outcome-based examinations. Before being issued any airframe and/or powerplant certificate, all applicants must demonstrate the minimum level of knowledge and skills for the certificate or rating sought.

Skill tests are significant as they measure the applicant's ability to logically think and objectively apply their knowledge, while demonstrating the physical skills that enable them to carry out aircraft maintenance in a professional and safe manner.

Satisfactory demonstration of each skill test is evidence the applicant meets the acceptable degree of competency for the certificate or rating sought.

This PTS is available for download, free of charge, at:

www.faa.gov

Comments regarding this PTS should be sent to:

AFS630comments@faa.gov

-OR-

U.S. Department of Transportation
Federal Aviation Administration
Regulatory Support Division
Airman Testing Standards Branch, AFS-630
P.O. Box 25082
Oklahoma City, OK 73125

Practical Test Standard Concept

Title 49 U.S. Code, Subtitle VII, Chapter 447 is the foundation for the FAA's safety regulations, and provides flexibility through FAA Order 8900.2, General Aviation Airman Designee Handbook, to examine and issue an airman certificate. This order is policy and mandatory standardized procedures for those who administer all aviation mechanic oral and practical tests.

NOTE: A designee conducting an oral and/or practical test must not test more than one applicant at a time, unless authorized in accordance with FAA Order 8900.1, *Flight Standards Information Management System* and FAA Order 8900.2.

Definitions within:

- **Competency**—a combination of skills, knowledge, and attitudes required to perform a task to the prescribed standard.
- **Knowledge** (oral)—elements are indicated by use of the words *"Exhibits knowledge in...."*
- **Skill**—(practical) elements are indicated by the use of the words *"Demonstrates the skill to perform...."*

This practical test book is a variety of technical projects or tasks containing subject areas included in the FAA written knowledge test as the current minimum required curriculum, which is prescribed in Title 14 of the Code of Federal Regulations (14 CFR) part 147 appendices.

Compliance with these procedures makes certain that airman applicants meet a satisfactory level of competency and workmanship required for certification.

Every applicant is required to demonstrate a minimum satisfactorily competency level, regardless of their previous education background.

Adherence to the following standards is mandatory when evaluating an applicant's test performance for an FAA Airframe and/or Powerplant Certificate:

- International Civil Aviation Organization (ICAO) Annex 1: 4.2.1.5
- 14 CFR part 65, section 65.79
- FAA Order 8900.2

All applicants for a FAA aviation mechanic certificate must qualify by meeting the prescribed requirements as stated in 14 CFR part 65, section 65.77. They must additionally pass a written knowledge test, and the oral and practical tests for the certificate and/or rating sought, in accordance with the following standards:

- ICAO Annex 1: 4.2.1.3
- 14 CFR part 65, section 65.77

FAA written knowledge tests contain topics that include the construction and maintenance of aircraft, relevant FAA regulations, basic principles for installation and maintenance of propellers, and powerplants, depending on the certificate and rating sought, based on the following standards:

- ICAO Annex 1: 4.2.1.2
- 14 CFR part 65, section 65.75

Aviation maintenance instructors and applicants should find these standards helpful during training and preparing for the skill test, which are required under 14 CFR part 65, section 65.79.

Reference List

14 CFR part 1	Definitions and Abbreviations
14 CFR part 3	General Requirements
14 CFR part 21	Certification Procedures for Products and Parts
14 CFR part 39	Airworthiness Directives
14 CFR part 43	Maintenance, Preventive Maintenance Rebuilding and Alteration
14 CFR part 45	Identification and Registration Marking
14 CFR part 47	Aircraft Registration
14 CFR part 65	Certification: Airmen Other Than Flight Crewmembers
14 CFR part 91	Air Traffic and General Operating Rules
AC 20-62E	Eligibility, Quality, and Identification of Aeronautical Replacement Parts
AC 21-12B	Application for U.S. Airworthiness Certificate
AC 23-21	Airworthiness Compliance Checklist Used to Substantiate Major Alteration for Small Airplanes
AC 23.1309-1E	System Safety Analysis and Assessment for Part 23 Airplanes
AC 39-7C	Airworthiness Directives
AC 43.9C	Maintenance Records
AC 43.9-1F	Instructions for Completion of FAA Form 337

AC 43-206	Inspection, Prevention, Control and Repair or Corrosion on Avionics Equipment
AC 43-210	Standardized Procedures for Requesting Field Approval of Data, Major Alteration and Repairs
AC 43.13-1B	Acceptable Methods, Techniques and Practices A/C Inspection & Repair
AC 43.13-2B	Acceptable Methods, Techniques and Practices-Aircraft Alterations
FAA-H-8083-1	Aircraft Weight and Balance Handbook
FAA-H-8083-30	Aviation Maintenance Technician Handbook—General
FAA-H-8083-31	Aviation Maintenance Technician Handbook—Airframe
ICAO	International Civil Aviation Organization Annex 1, Personnel Licensing

Each subject area has an objective. The objective lists the important knowledge and skill elements that must be utilized by the examiner in planning and administering aviation mechanic tests, and that applicants must be prepared to satisfactorily perform.

EXAMINER is used in this standard to denote either the FAA Inspector or FAA Designated Mechanic Examiner (DME) who conducts the practical test.

Use of the Practical Test Standards

The FAA requires that all practical tests be conducted in accordance with the appropriate Aviation Mechanic Practical Test Standards and the policies and procedures set forth in the current revision of FAA Order 8900.2.

When using this practical test book, the examiner must evaluate the applicant's knowledge and skill in sufficient depth to determine that the objective for each subject area element selected is met. If the element selected in one subject area has already been evaluated in another area, they need not be repeated. For example the applicant need not be evaluated in SUBJECT AREA H. MATHEMATICS, ELEMENT **H10.** Add, subtract, multiply, and divide positive and negative numbers. (Level 3) if that ELEMENT was sufficiently observed during the completion of SUBJECT AREA C. WEIGHT AND BALANCE, ELEMENT **C4.** Compute forward and aft loaded c.g. (Level 3).

An applicant is not permitted to know before testing begins which selections in each subject area are to be included in his/her test. Therefore, an applicant should be well prepared in *all* oral and skill areas included in the practical test standard.

Further information and requirements for conducting a practical test is contained in FAA Order 8900.2.

Aviation Mechanic Practical Test Prerequisites

All applicants must have met the prescribed experience requirements as stated in 14 CFR part 65, section 65.77. (See FAA Order 8900.2 for information about testing under the provisions of 14 CFR part 65, section 65.80.)

Examiner Responsibility

All applicants must demonstrate an approval for return to service standard, where applicable and demonstrate the ability to locate and apply the required reference materials, where applicable. In instances where an approval for return to service standard cannot be achieved, the applicant must be able to explain why the return to service standard was not met (e.g., when tolerances are outside of a product's limitations).

The examiner must personally observe all practical projects performed by the applicant. The examiner who conducts the practical test is responsible for determining that the applicant meets acceptable standards of knowledge and skill in the assigned subject areas within the appropriate practical test standard. Since there is no formal division between the knowledge and skill portions of the practical test, this becomes an ongoing process throughout the test.

The following terms may be reviewed with the applicant prior to, or during, element assignment.

1. **Inspect**—means to examine by sight and/or touch (with or without inspection enhancing tools/equipment).
2. **Check**—means to verify proper operation.
3. Troubleshoot—means to analyze and identify malfunctions.
4. **Service**—means to perform functions that assure continued operation.
5. **Repair**—means to correct a defective condition. Repair of an airframe or powerplant system includes component replacement and adjustment, but not component repair.
6. **Overhaul**—means to disassemble, inspect, repair as necessary, and check.

Performance Levels

The following is a detailed description of the meaning of each level.

Level 1

- Know basic facts and principles.
- Be able to find information and follow directions and written instructions.
- Locate methods, procedures, instructions, and reference material.
- Interpretation of information not required.
- No skill demonstration is required.

Example:

Z3b. Locate specified nondestructive testing methods. (Level 1)

Performance Standard: The applicant will locate information for nondestructive testing.

Level 2

- Know and understand principles, theories, and concepts.
- Be able to find and interpret maintenance data and information, and perform basic operations using appropriate data, tools, and equipment.
- A high level of skill is not required.

Example:

Z3c. Detect electrical leakage in electrical connections, terminal strips, and cable harness (at least 10 will have leakage faults). (Level 2)

Performance Standard: Using appropriate maintenance data and a multimeter, the applicant will identify items with leakage faults.

Level 3 (This is the approval for return to service standards).

- Know, understand, and apply facts, principles, theories, and concepts.
- Understand how they relate to the total operation and maintenance of aircraft.
- Be able to make independent and accurate airworthiness judgments.
- Perform all skill operations to a return-to-service standard using appropriate data, tools, and equipment. Inspections are performed in accordance with acceptable or approved data.
- A fairly high skill level is required.

Example:

Z3e. Check control surface travel. (Level 3)

Performance Standard: Using type certificate data sheets and the manufacturer's service manual, the applicant will measure the control surface travel, compare the travel to the maintenance data, and determine if the travel is within limits.

Satisfactory Performance

The practical test is passed if the applicant demonstrates the prescribed proficiency in the assigned elements in each subject area to the required standard. Applicants shall not be expected to memorize all mathematical formulas that may be required in the performance of various elements in this practical test standard. However, where relevant, applicants must be able to locate and apply necessary formulas to obtain correct solutions.

Unsatisfactory Performance

If the applicant does not meet the standards of any of the elements performed (knowledge or skill elements), the associated subject area is failed, and thus the practical test is failed. The examiner or the applicant may discontinue testing any time after the failure of a subject area. In any case, the applicant is entitled to credit for only those subject areas satisfactorily completed. See the current revision of FAA Order 8900.2 for further information about retesting and allowable credit for subject areas satisfactorily completed.

Typical areas of unsatisfactory performance and grounds for disqualification include the following.

1. Any action or lack of action by the applicant that requires corrective intervention by the examiner for reasons of safety.
2. Failure to follow acceptable or approved maintenance procedures while performing skill (practical) projects.
3. Exceeding tolerances stated in the maintenance instructions.
4. Failure to recognize improper procedures.
5. The inability to perform to a return to service standard, where applicable.
6. Inadequate knowledge in any of the subject areas.

SECTION II—AIRFRAME STRUCTURES

A. WOOD STRUCTURES

REFERENCES: FAA-H-8083-31; AC 43-13 1B.

Objective.   To determine that the applicant:

1. Exhibits knowledge in, as a minimum, two of the following elements—

    a. inspection tools for wood structures.
    b. inspection techniques and practices for wood structures.
    c. effects of moisture/humidity on wood.
    d. types and/or general characteristics of wood used in aircraft structures.
    e. permissible substitutes and/or other materials used in the construction and repair of wood structures.
    f. acceptable wood defects.
    g. non-acceptable wood defects.
    h. wood repair techniques and practices.

2. Demonstrates skill to perform, as a minimum, one of the following elements—

    A1.   Locate substitute wood material chart. (Level 1)
    A2.   Inspect aircraft wood structure or wood sample. (Level 3)
    A3.   Locate procedures for selecting glue used for wood structure repairs. (Level 1)
    A4.   Locate repair standard dimensions. (Level 1)
    A5.   Inspect a wood repair for airworthiness. (Level 3)
    A6.   Locate repair procedures for elongated bolt holes. (Level 1)
    A7.   Identify protective finishes. (Level 2)
    A8.   Identify wood defects. (Level 2)
    A9.   Determine acceptable repairs or limits for one or more specific defects. (Level 2)
    A10. List three types of wood used in aircraft structure. (Level 1)
    A11. Identify and select aircraft quality/acceptable wood. (Level 2)
    A12. Locate instructions for inspection of wood structures. (Level 1)
    A13. Locate instructions for inspection of plywood structure and/or wood repairs. (Level 1)
    A14. Locate wood spar and/or rib structure repair procedures. (Level 1)

B. AIRCRAFT COVERING

REFERENCES: FAA-H-8083-31; AC 43-13 1B.

Objective.   To determine that the applicant:

1. Exhibits knowledge in, as a minimum, two of the following elements—

    a. factors used in determining the proper type covering material.
    b. types of approved aircraft covering material.
    c. seams commonly used.
    d. covering textile terms.
    e. structure surface preparation.
    f. covering methods commonly used.
    g. covering means of attachment.
    h. areas on aircraft covering most susceptible to deterioration.
    i. aircraft covering preservation/restoration.
    j. inspection of aircraft covering.
    k. covering repair techniques and practices.

2. Demonstrates skill to perform, as a minimum, one of the following elements—

    B1.   Identify types of material used in aircraft covering. (Level 2)
    B2.   Locate procedures for applying fabric. (Level 1)
    B3.   Locate inspection requirements for fabric. (Level 1)
    B4.   Locate repair instructions for fabric or fiberglass. (Level 1)
    B5.   Locate test procedures for fabric. (Level 1)
    B6.   Describe needed repairs for a damaged fabric. (Level 1)
    B7.   Locate fabric critical areas. (Level 1)
    B8.   Locate instructions for a hand-sewn fabric seam. (Level 1)
    B9.   Locate instructions for repairing a sewn fabric tear. (Level 1)
    B10. Locate instructions for a splice lacing cord. (Level 1)
    B11. Locate instructions for tying a modified seine knot. (Level 1)
    B12. Locate instructions for the repair of a wing trailing edge fabric damage. (Level 1)
    B13. Determine the applicability of installing supplemental type certificate (STC) covering materials on a given aircraft. (Level 2
    B14. Locate instructions for preparing a fabric sample for laboratory testing. (Level 1)
    B15. Locate the general requirements for making doped and lapped seams. (Level 1)
    B16. Locate instructions for the repair and replacement of fabric on a fabric-covered surface using screws, special fasteners, or mechanical methods. (Level 1)
    B17. Locate instructions for installing ventilation/drainage grommets on a fabric surface. (Level 1)
    B18. Determine the classification of a repair on a fabric-covered surface. (Level 2)

C.   AIRCRAFT FINISHES

REFERENCES: FAA-H-8083-31; AC 43-13 1B; 14 CFR part 45.
Objective. To determine that the applicant:

1. Exhibits knowledge in, as a minimum, two of the following elements—

   a.   protection of airframe structures.
   b.   primer materials.
   c.   topcoat materials.
   d.   surface preparation for a desired finishing material.
   e.   effects of ambient conditions on finishing materials.
   f.   effects of improper surface preparation on finishing materials.
   g.   regulatory requirements for registration markings.
   h.   inspection of aircraft finishes.
   i.   safety practices/precautions when using finishing materials.
   j.   fungicidal, butyrate, and/or nitrate dopes.
   k.   finishing materials application techniques and practices.
   l.   where necessary, balance considerations after refinishing.

2. Demonstrates skill to perform, as a minimum, one of the following elements—

   C1.   Determine location and/or size requirements for aircraft registration numbers. (Level 2)
   C2.   Prepare composite surface for painting. (Level 2)
   C3.   Identify finishing materials and thinners. (Level 2)
   C4.   Layout and mask an aircraft identification marking ("N" number). (Level 2)
   C5.   Apply dope by brush to a fabric surface. (Level 2)
   C6.   Apply dope with a spray gun. (Level 3)
   C7.   Prepare metal surface for painting. (Level 2)
   C8.   Spray paint metal surfaces. (Level 2)
   C9.   Inspect doped fabric finish. (Level 2)
   C10. Inspect acrylic nitrocellulose lacquer finish. (Level 2)
   C11. Identify paint finish defects. (Level 2)
   C12. Determine what paint system can be used on a given aircraft. (Level 2)
   C13. Apply etch solution and conversion coating. (Level 2)
   C14. Determine if control surfaces require rebalancing. (Level 2)
   C15. Identify types of protective finishes. (Level 2)

FAA-S-8081-27A

D. SHEET METAL AND NON-METALLIC STRUCTURES

REFERENCES: FAA-H-8083-31; AC 43-13 1B.

Objective. To determine that the applicant:

1. Exhibits knowledge in, as a minimum, two of the following elements—

    a. inspection/testing of sheet metal structures.
    b. types of sheet metal defects.
    c. selection of sheet metal.
    d. layout, and/or forming of sheet metal.
    e. selection of rivets.
    f. rivet layout.
    g. rivet installation.
    h. inspection/testing of composite structures.
    i. types of composite structure defects.
    j. composite structure fiber, core, and/or matrix materials.
    k. composite materials storage practices and shelf life.
    l. composite structure repair methods, techniques, and practices.
    m. window inspection/types of defects.
    n. window material storage and handling.
    o. window installation procedures.
    p. care and maintenance of windows.
    q. window temporary and/or permanent repairs.
    r. maintenance safety practices/precautions for sheet metal, and/or composite materials/structures, and/or windows.

2. Demonstrates skill to perform, as a minimum, one of the following elements—

    D1. Prepare and install a patch for damage to an aircraft or component. (Level 3)
    D2. Make a drawing of a repair and determine the number of rivets and size required for the repair. (Level 3)
    D3. Remove a patch that was installed with rivets. (Level 3)
    D4. Trim and form a piece of sheet metal to fit into a prepared area. (Level 3)
    D5. Fabricate a complex aluminum part in accordance with a drawing. (Level 3)
    D6. Determine a rivet pattern for a specific repair given pitch, gauge, and edge distance. (Level 2)
    D7. Install special fasteners of at least 2 different types. (Level 2)

D8. Perform metallic ring test on bonded structure. (Level 2)

D9. Countersink holes in sheet metal to .010 tolerance. (Level 2)

D10. Inspect composite, plastic, or glass-laminated structures. (Level 3)

D11. Inspect acrylic type windshields. (Level 3)

D12. Identify window enclosure materials. (Level 2)

D13. Inspect pilot seat and seatbelt to include technical standard order (TSO) markings. (Level 3)

D14. Perform a repair on a damaged aluminum sheet. (Level 3)

E. WELDING

REFERENCES: FAA-H-8083-31; AC 43-13 1B.

Objective. To determine that the applicant:

1. Exhibits knowledge in, as a minimum, two of the following elements—

    a. flame welding gasses.
    b. storage/handling of welding gasses.
    c. flame welding practices and techniques.
    d. inert-gas welding practices and techniques.
    e. purpose and types of shielding gasses.
    f. characteristics of acceptable welds.
    g. characteristics of unacceptable welds.
    h. types of steel tubing welding repairs.
    i. procedures for weld repairs.
    j. soldering preparation, types of solder, and/or flux usage.
    k. welding and/or soldering safety practices/precautions.

2. Demonstrates skill to perform, as a minimum, one of the following elements—

    E1. Solder aircraft wire and connectors. (Level 2)
    E2. Select torch tips. (Level 2)
    E3. Select welding rods. (Level 2)
    E4. Adjust oxyacetylene flame to neutral appearance. (Level 2)
    E5. Perform a silver solder joint. (Level 2)
    E6. Braze a lap joint. (Level 2)
    E7. Locate the method of cleaning magnesium in preparation for welding. (Level 1)
    E8. Fabricate a weld patch (diamond patch). (Level 2)
    E9. Perform oxyacetylene butt welds. (Level 2)
    E10. Demonstrate electric arc welding. (Level 2)
    E11. Select repair procedure for tubular structure. (Level 1)
    E12. Inspect and check welds. (Level 2)

F.   ASSEMBLY AND RIGGING

REFERENCES: FAA-H-8083-31; AC 43-13 1B.

Objective. To determine that the applicant:

1.   Exhibits knowledge in, as a minimum, two of the following elements—

    a.   control cable.
    b.   control cable maintenance.
    c.   cable connectors.
    d.   cable guides.
    e.   control stops.
    f.   push pull tubes.
    g.   torque tubes.
    h.   bell cranks.
    i.   flutter and flight control balance.
    j.   rigging of airplane or rotorcraft flight controls.
    k.   airplane or rotorcraft flight controls and/or stabilizer systems.
    l.   types of rotorcraft rotor systems.
    m.   rotor vibrations.
    n.   rotor blade tracking.
    o.   aircraft jacking procedures.
    p.   jacking safety practices/precautions.

2.   Demonstrates skill to perform, as a minimum, one of the following elements—

    F1.   Locate the procedures needed to rig a helicopter. (Level 1)
    F2.   Locate causes of vertical vibration in a two blade helicopter rotor system. (Level 1)
    F3.   Locate helicopter rotor blade tracking procedures. (Level 1)
    F4.   Identify fixed-wing aircraft rigging adjustment locations. (Level 2)
    F6.   Identify control surfaces that provide movement about an aircraft's axes. (Level 2)
    F7.   Locate leveling methods and procedures. (Level 1)
    F8.   Verify alignment of an empennage. (Level 3)
    F9.   Verify alignment of landing gear. (Level 3)
    F10.   Inspect a primary and secondary flight control surface. (Level 3)
    F11.   Remove and/or reinstall a primary flight control surface. (Level 3)
    F12.   Assemble aircraft components. (Level 3)
    F13.   Inspect primary control cables. (Level 3)
    F14.   Install swaged cable terminals. (Level 3)
    F15.   Remove and reinstall a primary flight control cable. (Level 3)
    F16.   Adjust push-pull flight control systems. (Level 3)
    F17.   Balance a flight control surface. (Level 3)
    F18.   Locate jacking procedures. (Level 1)
    F19.   Locate jacking points. (Level 1)

G.   AIRFRAME INSPECTION

REFERENCES: FAA-H-8083-31; AC 43-13 1B.

Objective. To determine that the applicant:

1. Exhibits knowledge in, as a minimum, two of the following elements—

    a. one or more required inspections under 14 CFR part 91.
    b. maintenance requirements under 14 CFR part 43.
    c. inspection requirements under 14 CFR part 43.
    d. requirements for complying with airworthiness directives.
    e. compliance with service letters, instructions for continued airworthiness, and/or bulletins.
    f. maintenance record requirements under 14 CFR part 43.
    g. maintenance record requirements under 14 CFR part 91.

2. Demonstrates skill to perform, as a minimum, one of the following elements—

    G1. Check a given aircraft for airworthiness directive compliance. (Level 3)
    G2. Perform a portion of a 100-hour/annual inspection in accordance with Part 43, Appendix D. (Level 3)
    G3. Enter results of a 100-hour inspection in maintenance records. (Level 3)
    G4. Perform a portion of the conformity inspection on an engine, airframe, or propeller. (Level 3)
    G5. Determine when the next annual and/or 100-hour inspection is required on a specific aircraft. (Level 2)
    G6. Determine if a particular repetitive airworthiness directive has been accomplished. (Level 3)
    G7. Provide a checklist for conducting a 100-hour inspection. (Level 2)

SECTION III—AIRFRAME SYSTEMS AND COMPONENTS

K. AIRCRAFT LANDING GEAR SYSTEMS

REFERENCES: FAA-H-8083-31; AC 43-13 1B.

Objective. To determine that the applicant:

1. Exhibits knowledge in, as a minimum, two of the following elements—

    a. landing gear strut servicing/lubrication.
    b. landing gear steering systems.
    c. landing gear retraction/extension systems.
    d. landing gear inspection.
    e. brake assembly inspection.
    f. wheel and tire construction
    g. tire mounting.
    h. wheel and tire inspection.
    i. wheel bearing inspection.
    j. tire storage, care, and/or servicing.
    k. landing gear and/or tire and wheel safety
         practices/precautions.

2. Demonstrates skill to perform, as a minimum, one of the following elements—

    K1. Service landing gear air/oil shock strut. (Level 3)
    K2. Bleed air from a hydraulic brake system. (Level 3)
    K3. Troubleshoot hydraulic brake systems. (Level 3)
    K4. Remove, inspect, service, and/or reinstall a wheel assembly. (Level 3)
    K5. Demount, inspect, and/or reinstall a tire on a wheel. (Level 3)
    K6. Remove, inspect, and/or install a wheel brake assembly. (Level 3)
    K7. Inspect a tire for defects. (Level 3)
    K8. Repair a defective tube. (Level 3)
    K9. Locate tire storage practices. (Level 1)
    K10. Replace a tire or tube valve core and inspect for leaks. (Level 3)
    K11. Remove and replace brake linings. (Level 3)
    K12. Replace air/oil shock strut air valve. (Level 3)
    K13. Troubleshoot an air/oil shock strut. (Level 3)
    K14. Service a nosewheel shimmy damper. (Level 3)
    K15. Adjust nosewheel steering system. (Level 3)
    K16. Inspect landing gear alignment. (Level 3)
    K17. Replace master brake cylinder packing seals. (Level 3)
    K18. Troubleshoot landing gear retract system. (Level 3)
    K19. Troubleshoot aircraft steering system. (Level 3)
    K20. Inspect a brake for serviceability. (Level 3)

L.   HYDRAULIC AND PNEUMATIC POWER SYSTEMS

REFERENCES: FAA-H-8083-31; AC 43-13 1B.

Objective. To determine that the applicant:

1.   Exhibits knowledge in, as a minimum, two of the following elements—

a.   hydraulic and/or pneumatic system, and/or system component(s) function/operation.
b.   servicing, function, and/or operation of accumulators.
c.   types of hydraulic/pneumatic seals and/or fluid/seal compatibility.
d.   hydraulic/pneumatic seal maintenance procedures.
e.   types of hydraulic/pneumatic filters and/or filter operation.
f.   filter maintenance procedures.
g.   pressure regulators and valves.
h.   servicing hydraulic and/or pneumatic systems.
i.   types/identification and/or characteristics of various hydraulics fluids used in aircraft.
j.   hydraulic/pneumatic system safety practices/precautions.

2.   Demonstrates skill to perform, as a minimum, one of the following elements—

L1.   Identify different types of hydraulic fluids. (Level 2)
L2.   Identify different packing seals. (Level 2)
L3.   Install seals in a hydraulic component. (Level 3)
L4.   Remove and install a selector valve. (Level 3)
L5.   Check a pressure regulator and adjust as necessary. (Level 3)
L6.   Remove, clean, and install a hydraulic system filter. (Level 3)
L7.   Service a hydraulic system accumulator. (Level 3)
L8.   Service a hydraulic system reservoir. (Level 3)
L9.   Remove, install, and check an engine-driven hydraulic pump. (Level 3)
L10.   Troubleshoot hydraulic power system. (Level 3)
L11.   Purge air from a hydraulic system. (Level 3)
L12.   Remove and/or install a system pressure relief valve. (Level 3)
L13.   Troubleshoot a hydraulic power system leak. (Level 3)
L14.   Troubleshoot a pneumatic power system leak. (Level 3)
L15.   Service pneumatic brake system air bottles. (Level 3)
L16.   Inspect a pneumatic air bottle for condition and determine service life (hydrostatic testing). (Level 2)
L18.   Adjust a pneumatic power system relief valve. (Level 3)
L19.   Locate fluid servicing instructions and identify/select fluid for a given aircraft. (Level 2)

M. CABIN ATMOSPHERE CONTROL SYSTEMS

REFERENCES: FAA-H-8083-31; AC 43-13 1B.

Objective. To determine that the applicant:

1. Exhibits knowledge in, as a minimum, two of the following elements—

   a. exhaust heat exchanger and/or system component(s) function, operation, and/or inspection procedures.
   b. combustion heater and/or system component(s) function, operation, and/or inspection procedures.
   c. vapor-cycle system and/or system component(s) operation, servicing and/or inspection procedures.
   d. air-cycle system and/or system component(s) operation and/or inspection procedures.
   e. cabin pressurization and/or system component(s) operation and/or inspection procedures.
   f. types of oxygen systems and/or oxygen system component(s) operation.
   g. oxygen system maintenance procedures.

2. Demonstrates skill to perform, as a minimum, one of the following elements—

   M1. Locate procedures for troubleshooting a non-operational surface combustion heater. (Level 1)
   M2. Locate the procedures for protecting a freon system from contamination during replacement of a component. (Level 1)
   M3. Locate sources of contamination in a freon system. (Level 1)
   M4. Locate the procedures for checking a combustion heater fuel system for leaks. (Level 1)
   M5. Identify and describe the units in a freon system in relation to each other. (Level 2)
   M6. Locate the servicing procedures for a vapor-cycle air conditioning system. (Level 1)
   M7. Locate the inspection requirements for a cabin heater system equipped with an exhaust heat exchanger. (Level 1)
   M8. Locate the procedures for inspecting an outflow valve in a pressurization system. (Level 1)
   M9. Locate operating instructions for a freon system. (Level 1)
   M10. Locate the negative pressure relief valve. (Level 1)
   M11. Check an oxygen system for leaks. (Level 2)
   M12. Inspect an oxygen system. (Level 2)
   M13. Service an oxygen system. (Level 2)
   M14. Locate troubleshooting procedures for an oxygen system. (Level 1)
   M15. Locate instructions for the Inspection of a pressurization system. (Level 1)

N. AIRCRAFT INSTRUMENT SYSTEMS

REFERENCES: FAA-H-8083-31; AC 43-13 1B.

Objective. To determine that the applicant:

1. Exhibits knowledge in, as a minimum, two of the following elements—

    a. magnetic compass operation.
    b. magnetic compass swinging procedures.

    c. gyroscopic instrument(s) purpose and operation.
    d. vacuum/pressure and/or electrically operated instrument system operation.
    e. vacuum/pressure and/or electricity operated instrument system maintenance procedures.
    f. pitot and/or static instruments purpose and operation.
    g. pitot and/or static system operation.
    h. 14 CFR parts 43 and/or 91 requirements for static system checks.
    i. aircraft instrument range markings.

2. Demonstrates skill to perform, as a minimum, one of the following elements—

    N1. Remove and install instruments. (Level 3)
    N2. Install range marks on an instrument glass. (Level 3)
    N3. Determine barometric pressure using an altimeter. (Level 2)
    N4. Check pitot-static heat for proper operation. (Level 2)
    N5. Check for proper indication of a manifold pressure gage. (Level 2)
    N6. Perform a pitot-static system leak test. (Level 2)
    N7. Apply instrument glass slippage marks. (Level 2)
    N8. Locate instructions for the inspection of a magnetic compass. (Level 1)
    N9. Locate procedures for troubleshooting a vacuum operated turn-and-bank instruments. (Level 1)
    N10. Identify an electric attitude indicator. (Level 2)
    N11. Select proper altimeter for installation on a given aircraft. (Level 2)
    N12. Locate a synchro-type indicating system. (Level 2)
    N13. Locate a vacuum pump. (Level 2)
    N14. Remove and install a heated pitot tube. (Level 3)
    N15. Identify exhaust gas temperature system components. (Level 2)

N16. Explain the troubleshooting procedures for an electrical resistance thermometer system. (Level 2)

N17. Service a vacuum system filter. (Level 2)

N18. Check an altimeter system for certification for instrument flight rules (IFR). (Level 2)

N19. Identify an aircraft vacuum system. (Level 2)

N20. Adjust gyro/instrument air pressure. (Level 2)

N21. Inspect a cylinder head temperature indicating system. (Level 2)

N22. Locate and explain troubleshooting procedures for a directional gyro system malfunction. (Level 2)

N23. Locate the alternate air source on an aircraft. (Level 2)

O. COMMUNICATION AND NAVIGATION SYSTEMS

REFERENCES: FAA-H-8083-31; AC 43-13 1B; 14 CFR part 91.

Objective. To determine that the applicant:

1. Exhibits knowledge in, as a minimum, two of the following elements—

   a. 14 CFR part 91 emergency locator transmitter (ELT) maintenance requirements.
   b. 14 CFR part 91 ELT record keeping requirements.
   c. checking/inspecting coaxial cable.
   d. coaxial cable installation and/or routing requirements.
   e. communication and/or navigation systems commonly used.
   f. proper installation of a com/nav radio in an existing radio rack.
   g. means of identification of commonly used communication and/or navigation antennas.
   h. autopilot system basic components and/or sensing elements.
   i. static discharger function and operation.
   j. static discharger maintenance procedures.

2. Demonstrates skill to perform, as a minimum, one of the following elements—

   O1. Locate operating instructions for an autopilot system. (Level 1)
   O2. Locate autopilot inspection procedures. (Level 1)
   O3. List autopilot major components. (Level 2)
   O4. Locate and identify navigation and/or communication antennas. (Level 2)
   O5. Check very high frequency (VHF) communications for operation. (Level 2)
   O6. Inspect a coaxial cable installation for security. (Level 3)
   O7. Check an emergency locator transmitter for operation. (Level 2)
   O8. Inspect ELT batteries for expiration date. (Level 2)
   O9. Inspect electronic equipment mounting base for security and condition. (Level 2)
   O10. Inspect electronic equipment shock mount bonding jumpers for resistance. (Level 2)
   O11. Inspect static discharge wicks for security and/or resistance. (Level 2)
   O12. Inspect a radio installation for security. (Level 2)
   O13. Locate weather radar operating procedures. (Level 1)
   O14. Identify transponder transmission line. (Level 2)
   O15. Locate installation procedures for antennas including mounting and coaxial connections. (Level 1)
   O16. Make a list of required placards for communication and navigation avionic equipment. (Level 2)

P. AIRCRAFT FUEL SYSTEMS

REFERENCES: FAA-H-8083-31; AC 43-13 1B.

Objective. To determine that the applicant:

1. Exhibits knowledge in, as a minimum, two of the following elements—

    a. fuel system strainer servicing.
    b. construction characteristics of one or more types of fuel tanks.
    c. fuel tank maintenance procedures.
    d. fuel line routing/installation requirements.
    e. hazards associated with fuel system maintenance.
    f. types, characteristics, and/or operation of fuel systems and/or components thereof.
    g. characteristics, and/or operation of fuel jettison systems and/or components thereof.

2. Demonstrates skill to perform, as a minimum, one of the following elements—

    P1. Inspect a metal fuel tank. (Level 3)
    P2. Inspect a bladder fuel tank. (Level 3)
    P3. Inspect an integral fuel tank. (Level 3)
    P4. Check manually operated fuel valves for proper operation and/or leaks. (Level 3)
    P5. Troubleshoot a fuel valve problem. (Level 3)
    P6. Drain fuel system sumps. (Level 3)
    P7. Service a fuel system strainer. (Level 3)
    P8. Locate instructions for the calibration of a direct reading fuel indicating system. (Level 1)
    P9. Inspect a remote indicating fuel quantity system. (Level 2)
    P10. Locate fuel system operating instructions. (Level 1)
    P11. Locate fuel system inspection procedures. (Level 1)
    P12. Locate fuel system crossfeed procedures. (Level 1)
    P13. Locate fuel system required placards. (Lovol 2)
    P14. Locate fuel system defueling procedures. (Level 1)
    P15. Troubleshoot fuel pressure warning system. (Level 3)
    P16. Locate troubleshooting procedures for fuel temperature systems. (Level 1)
    P17. Remove and/or install a fuel quantity transmitter. (Level 3)
    P18. Troubleshoot aircraft fuel systems. (Level 3)
    P19. Remove and install a fuel selector valve. (Level 3)

Q. AIRCRAFT ELECTRICAL SYSTEMS

REFERENCES: FAA-H-8083-31; AC 43-13 1B.

Objective. To determine that the applicant:

1. Exhibits knowledge in, as a minimum, two of the following elements—

   a. factors to consider when selecting wire size for an aircraft circuit.
   b. routing and/or installation of electric wire or wire bundles.
   c. wire splicing.
   d. use of derating factors in switch selection.
   e. requirements for circuit protection devices.
   f. voltage regulator—purpose and operating characteristics.
   g. lighting and/or lighting system components.
   h. electric motor operation and/or motor components.
   i. constant speed drive (CSD) and/or integrated drive generator (IDG) systems and/or system components.
   j. airframe electrical system components.
   k. wiring defects and/or inspection.

2. Demonstrates skill to perform, as a minimum, one of the following elements—

   Q1. Select and install the appropriate type of wiring in a given electrical circuit. (Level 3)
   Q2. Select and install the appropriate type of electrical switches in a given circuit. (Level 3)
   Q3. Secure wire bundles. (Level 3)
   Q4. Select and install fuses and/or circuit protectors in a given aircraft electrical system. (Level 3)
   Q5. Determine an electrical load in a given aircraft system. (Level 3)
   Q6. Install bonding jumpers. (Level 3)
   Q7. Splice electrical wire. (Level 3)
   Q8. Check output voltage of a direct current (DC) generator. (Level 3)
   Q9. Adjust voltage regulators. (Level 3)
   Q10. Troubleshoot an electrical circuit with an open or short. (Level 3)
   Q11. Check the resistance of an electrical system component. (Level 2)
   Q12. Check generator brush spring tension and/or service ability. (Level 2)

Q13. Inspect and check anti-collision, position, and/or landing lights for proper operation. (Level 3)

Q14. Identify components in an electrical system. (Level 2)

Q15. Identify cockpit lighting circuits. (Level 2)

Q16. Troubleshoot a DC electrical system supplied by an alternating current (AC) electrical system. (Level 3)

Q17. Identify components in an electrical schematic where AC is rectified to a DC voltage. (Level 2)

Q18. Visually identify and describe operation of components in a constant speed drive (CSD) or integrated drive generator (IDG). (Level 2)

R. POSITION AND WARNING SYSTEM

REFERENCES: FAA-H-8083-31; AC 43-13 1B.

Objective.   To determine that the applicant:

1. Exhibits knowledge in, as a minimum, two of the following elements—

    a. anti-skid system basic components.
    b. anti-skid system operating characteristics.
    c. takeoff warning system basic components.
    d. takeoff warning system function and operation.
    e. control-surface trim indicating system basic components and/or operating characteristics.
    f. landing gear position indicators.
    g. flap position indicators.
    h. landing gear warning system basic components and/or operating characteristics.
    i. checking and/or repairing a landing gear warning system.
    j. types of stall warning/lift detector systems and/or operating characteristics.
    k. common annunciator system indications.
    l. mach warning system indicator(s) and/or operating characteristics.

2. Demonstrates skill to perform, as a minimum, one of the following elements—

    R1. Identify landing gear position system components. (Level 2)
    R2. Troubleshoot landing gear position and/or warning systems. (Level 3)
    R3. Identify landing gear warning system components. (Level 2)
    R4. Locate procedures for checking operation of an anti-skid warning system. (Level 1)
    R5. Locate troubleshooting procedures for an anti-skid system. (Level 1)
    R6. Locate troubleshooting procedures for a takeoff warning system. (Level 1)
    R7. Inspect landing gear position indicating system. (Level 3)
    R8. Repair landing gear position indicating systems. (Level 3)
    R9. Describe the sequence of operation for a landing gear warning system. (Level 2)
    R10. Determine the adjustment requirements of a flap position warning system. (Level 2)

R11. Locate the adjustment procedures for a stall warning system. (Level 1)

R12. Remove, install, and/or adjust a landing gear down-lock switch. (Level 3)

R13. Check rigging and adjustment of landing gear up-lock. (Level 3)

R14. Locate procedures for checking pneumatic/bleed air overheat warning systems. (Level 1)

R15. Inspect an electrical brake control for proper operation. (Level 3)

S. ICE AND RAIN CONTROL SYSTEMS

REFERENCES: FAA-H-8083-31; AC 43-13 1B.

Objective.   To determine that the applicant:

1. Exhibits knowledge in, as a minimum, two of the following elements—

    a. aircraft icing causes/effects.
    b. ice detection systems.
    c. anti-ice and/or deice areas.
    d. anti-ice and/or deice methods commonly used.
    e. checking and/or troubleshooting a pitot-static anti-ice system.
    f. anti-icing and/or de-icing system components/operation.
    g. anti-icing and/or de-icing system maintenance.
    h. types of rain removal systems and/or operating characteristics.

2. Demonstrates skill to perform, as a minimum, one of the following elements—

    S1. Inspect a pneumatic deicer boot. (Level 3)
    S2. Perform operational check of pneumatic deicer boot system to determine sequence and timing.
    (Level 2)
    S3. Clean a pneumatic deicer boot. (Level 2)
    S4. Check an electrically-heated pitot tube system. (Level 2)
    S5. Locate procedures for troubleshooting an electrically-heated pitot system. (Level 1)
    S6. Check an electrically heated water drain system. (Level 2)
    S7. Inspect thermal anti-ice systems. (Level 2)
    S8. Check an electrically-heated windshield. (Level 2)
    S9. Inspect an electrically-operated windshield wiper system.
    (Level 2)
    S10. Check an electrically or hydraulically-operated windshield wiper system. (Level 2)
    S11. Replace blades on a windshield wiper system. (Level 2)
    S12. Check pneumatic rain removal system. (Level 2)
    S13. Check a rain repellent system. (Level 2)
    S14. Locate inspection procedures for chemical rain protection of a windscreen. (Level 1)

T. FIRE PROTECTION SYSTEMS

REFERENCES: FAA-H-8083-31; AC 43-13 1B.

Objective. To determine that the applicant:

1. Exhibits knowledge in, as a minimum, two of the following elements—

   a. fire and/or smoke detection system(s) or system components.
   b. fire extinguishing system(s) and/or system components.
   c. fire and/or smoke detection system operating characteristics.
   d. fire extinguishing system operating characteristics.
   e. determining proper container pressure for an installed fire extinguisher system.
   f. maintenance procedures for fire detection and/or extinguishing system(s) and/or system component(s).
   g. inspecting and/or checking a fire detection/overheat system.
   h. inspecting and/or checking a smoke and/or toxic gas detection system.
   i. troubleshooting a fire detection and/or extinguishing system.

2. Demonstrates skill to perform, as a minimum, one of the following elements—

   T1. Locate inspection procedures for carbon monoxide detectors. (Level 1)
   T2. Locate procedures for checking a smoke detection system. (Level 1)
   T3. Locate the procedures for inspecting a thermal switch fire detection system. (Level 1)
   T4. Inspect, check, troubleshoot, and/or repair a fire detection system. (Level 3)
   T5. Inspect a thermocouple fire warning system. (Level 1)
   T6. Check a continuous loop fire detection system. (Level 3)
   T7. Inspect a continuous loop fire detection system. (Level 2)
   T8. Inspect fire protection system CO2 cylinders. (Level 2)
   T9. Inspect conventional CO2 fire protection system. (Level 3)
   T10. Check a conventional CO2 fire-protection systems. (Level 2)
   T11. Check a fire protection system freon bottle charge pressure. (Level 3)
   T12. Inspect a high-rate-of-discharge fire-extinguisher system. (Level 2)
   T13. Locate troubleshooting procedures for a high-rate-of-discharge fire-extinguisher system. (Level 1)
   T14. Inspect Freon bottle discharge cartridge. (Level 3)
   T15. Check Freon bottle discharge circuit. (Level 2)
   T16. Inspect fire-extinguisher bottle or cylinder for hydrostatic test date. (Level 3)

FAA-S-8081-27A

U.S. Department
of Transportation

**Federal Aviation
Administration**

FAA-S-8081-28A

AVIATION MECHANIC POWERPLANT

Practical Test Standards

July 2012

FLIGHT STANDARDS SERVICE
Washington, DC 20591

POWERPLANT

AVIATION MECHANIC POWERPLANT

PRACTICAL TEST STANDARDS

2012

FLIGHT STANDARDS SERVICE
Washington, D.C. 20591

NOTE

FAA-S-8081-28A, Aviation Mechanic Powerplant Practical Test Standards (PTS) supersedes FAA-S-8081-28 dated June 2003.

This PTS will be effective November 1, 2012.

MAJOR ENHANCEMENTS

- Removed the core competency element requirements (objective 2) for each subject area.
- There are now only 2 objectives for each subject area:
  - Objective 1: Exhibits knowledge in, oral elements.
  - Objective 2: Demonstrates skill to perform practical elements.
- Added and/or revised elements within objective 2 to expand the selection of projects for the DME.
- Added new subject area "M" Human Factors/Maintenance Resource Management (MRM).
- Revised introduction to include International Civil Aviation Organization (ICAO) references to aircraft maintenance performance, eligibility, skill, knowledge, and experience requirements.
- Updated references to FAA orders, instructional materials, and inspector guidance.

FOREWORD

This Aviation Mechanic Powerplant Practical Test Standards book has been published by the Federal Aviation Administration (FAA) to establish the standards for the Aviation Mechanic Powerplant Practical Test. The passing of this practical test is a required step toward obtaining the Aviation Mechanic Certificate with a Powerplant rating. **FAA inspectors and Designated Mechanic Examiners (DMEs) shall conduct practical tests in compliance with these standards.** Applicants should find these standards helpful in practical test preparation.

/s/ 7/30/2012
Raymond Towles, for

_____
John Allen, Director
Flight Standards Service

CONTENTS

INTRODUCTION

The Federal Aviation Administration (FAA) aircraft mechanic's oral and practical test(s) are outcome-based examinations. Before being issued any airframe and/or powerplant certificate, all applicants must demonstrate the minimum level of knowledge and skills for the rating sought.

Skill tests are significant as they measure the applicant's ability to logically think and objectively apply their knowledge, while demonstrating the physical skills that enable them to carry out aircraft maintenance in a professional and safe manner.

Satisfactory demonstration of each skill test is evidence the applicant meets the acceptable degree of competency for the certificate or rating sought.

This PTS is available for download, free of charge, at:

www.faa.gov

Comments regarding this PTS should be sent to:

AFS630comments@faa.gov

-OR-

U.S. Department of Transportation
Federal Aviation Administration
Regulatory Support Division
Airman Testing Standards Branch, AFS-630
P.O. Box 25082
Oklahoma City, OK 73125

Practical Test Standard Concept

Title 49 U.S. Code, Subpart III, Chapter 447 is the foundation for the FAA's safety regulations, and provides flexibility through FAA Order 8900.2, General Aviation Airman Designee Handbook, to examine and issue an airman certificate. This order is policy and mandatory standardized procedures for those who administer all aviation mechanic oral and practical tests.

NOTE: A designee conducting an oral and/or practical test must not test more than one applicant at a time, unless authorized in accordance with FAA Order 8900.1, *Flight Standards Information Management System* and FAA Order 8900.2.

Definitions within:

- **Competency**—a combination of skills, knowledge, and attitudes required to perform a task to the prescribed standard.
- **Knowledge** (oral)—elements are indicated by use of the words *"Exhibits knowledge in...."*
- **Skill**—(practical) elements are indicated by the use of the words *"Demonstrates the skill to perform...."*

This practical test book is a variety of technical projects or tasks containing subject areas included in the FAA written knowledge test as the current minimum required curriculum, which is prescribed in Title 14 of the Code of Federal Regulations (14 CFR) part 147 appendices.

Compliance with these procedures makes certain that airman applicants meet a satisfactory level of competency and workmanship required for certification.

Every applicant is required to demonstrate a minimum satisfactorily competency level, regardless of their previous education background.

Adherence to the following standards is mandatory when evaluating an applicant's test performance for an FAA Airframe and/or Powerplant Certificate:

- International Civil Aviation Organization (ICAO) Annex 1: 4.2.1.5
- 14 CFR part 65, section 65.79
- FAA Order 8900.2

All applicants for an FAA Aviation Mechanic Certificate must qualify by meeting the prescribed requirements as stated in 14 CFR part 65, section 65.77. They must additionally pass a written knowledge test, and the oral and practical tests for the certificate and/or rating sought, in accordance with the following standards:

- ICAO Annex 1: 4.2.1.3
- 14 CFR part 65, section 65.77

FAA written knowledge tests contain topics that include the construction and maintenance of aircraft, relevant FAA regulations, basic principles for installation and maintenance of propellers, and powerplants, depending on the certificate and rating sought, based on the following standards:

- ICAO Annex 1: 4.2.1.2
- 14 CFR part 65, section 65.75

Aviation maintenance instructors and applicants should find these standards helpful during training and preparing for the skill test, which are required under 14 CFR part 65, section 65.79.

Reference List:

14 CFR part 1	Definitions and Abbreviations
14 CFR part 3	General Requirements
14 CFR part 21	Certification Procedures for Products and Parts
14 CFR part 39	Airworthiness Directives
14 CFR part 43	Maintenance, Preventive Maintenance Rebuilding and Alteration
14 CFR part 45	Identification and Registration Marking
14 CFR part 47	Aircraft Registration
14 CFR part 65	Certification: Airmen Other Than Flight Crewmembers
14 CFR part 91	Air Traffic and General Operating Rules
AC 20-62E	Eligibility, Quality, and Identification of Aeronautical Replacement Parts
AC 39-7C	Airworthiness Directives
AC 43.13-1B	Acceptable Methods, Techniques and Practices A/C Inspection & Repair
AC 43.13-2B	Acceptable Methods, Techniques and Practices- Aircraft Alterations
FAA-H-8083-30	Aviation Maintenance Technician Handbook— General
FAA-H-8083-32	Aviation Maintenance Technician Handbook— Powerplant
ICAO	International Civil Aviation Organization Annex 1, *Personnel Licensing*

Each subject area has an objective. The objective lists the important knowledge and skill elements that must be utilized by the examiner in planning and administering aviation mechanic tests, and that applicants must be prepared to satisfactorily perform.

EXAMINER is used throughout this standard to denote either the FAA Inspector or FAA Designated Mechanic Examiner (DME) who conducts the practical test.

Use of the Practical Test Standards

The FAA requires that all practical tests be conducted in accordance with the appropriate Aviation Mechanic Practical Test Standard, and the policies and procedures set forth in the current revision of FAA Order 8900.2.

When using the practical test standards, the examiner must evaluate the applicant's knowledge and skill in sufficient depth to determine that the objective for each subject area element selected is met. If the element selected in one subject area has already been evaluated in another area, they need not be repeated. For example, the applicant need not be evaluated in SUBJECT AREA H. MATHEMATICS, ELEMENT **H10.** Add, subtract, multiply, and divide positive and negative numbers (Level 3). If that ELEMENT was sufficiently observed during the completion of SUBJECT AREA C. WEIGHT AND BALANCE, ELEMENT **C4.** Compute forward and aft loaded c.g. (Level 3).

An applicant is not permitted to know before testing begins which selections in each subject area are to be included in his/her test. Therefore, an applicant should be well prepared in **all** oral and skill areas included in the practical test standard.

Further information and requirements for conducting a practical test is contained in FAA Order 8900.2.

Aviation Mechanic Practical Test Prerequisites

All applicants must have met the prescribed experience requirements as stated in 14 CFR part 65, section 65.77 or be an authorized school student per 14 CFR part 65, section 65.80. (See FAA Order 8900.2 for information about testing under the provisions of 14 CFR part 65, section 65.80.)

Examiner Responsibility

All applicants must demonstrate an approval for return to service standard, where applicable and demonstrate the ability to locate and apply the required reference materials, where applicable. In instances where an approval for return to service standard cannot be achieved, the applicant must be able to explain why the return to service standard was not met (e.g., when tolerances are outside of a product's limitations).

The examiner must personally observe all practical projects performed by the applicant. The examiner who conducts the practical test is responsible for determining that the applicant meets acceptable standards of knowledge and skill in the assigned subject areas within the appropriate practical test standard. Since there is no formal division between the knowledge and skill portions of the practical test, this becomes an ongoing process throughout the test.

The following terms may be reviewed with the applicant prior to, or during, element assignment.

1. **Inspect**—means to examine by sight and/or touch (with or without inspection enhancing tools/equipment).
2. **Check**—means to verify proper operation.
3. **Troubleshoot**—means to analyze and identify malfunctions.
4. **Service**—means to perform functions that assure continued operation.
5. **Repair**—means to correct a defective condition. Repair of an airframe or powerplant system includes component replacement and adjustment, but not component repair.
6. **Overhaul**—means disassembled, cleaned, inspected, repaired as necessary, and reassembled.

Performance Levels

The following is a detailed description of the meaning of each level.

Level 1

- Know basic facts and principles.
- Be able to find information and follow directions and written instructions.
- Locate methods, procedures, instructions, and reference material.
- Interpretation of information not required.
- No skill demonstration is required.

Example:

Z3b. Locate specified nondestructive testing methods.(Level 1)

Performance Standard: The applicant will locate information for nondestructive testing.

Level 2

- Know and understand principles, theories, and concepts.
- Be able to find and interpret maintenance data and information, and perform basic operations using appropriate data, tools, and equipment.
- A high level of skill is not required.

Example:

Z3c. Detect electrical leakage in electrical connections, terminal strips, and cable harness (at least 10 will have leakage faults). (Level 2)

Performance Standard: Using appropriate maintenance data and a multimeter, the applicant will identify items with leakage faults.

Level 3 (This is the approval for return to service standards).

- Know, understand, and apply facts, principles, theories, and concepts.
- Understand how they relate to the total operation and maintenance of aircraft.
- Be able to make independent and accurate airworthiness judgments.
- Perform all skill operations to a return-to-service standard using appropriate data, tools, and equipment. Inspections are performed in accordance with acceptable or approved data.
- A fairly high skill level is required.

Example:

Z3e. Check control surface travel. (Level 3)

Performance Standard: Using type certificate data sheets and the manufacturer's service manual, the applicant will measure the control surface travel, compare the travel to the maintenance data, and determine if the travel is within limits.

Satisfactory Performance

The practical test is passed if the applicant demonstrates the prescribed proficiency in the assigned elements in each subject area to the required standard. Applicants shall not be expected to memorize all mathematical formulas that may be required in the performance of various elements in this practical test standard. However, where relevant, applicants must be able to locate and apply necessary formulas to obtain correct solutions.

Unsatisfactory Performance

If the applicant does not meet the standards of any of the elements performed (knowledge or skill elements), the associated subject area is failed, and thus the practical test is failed. The examiner or the applicant may discontinue testing any time after the failure of a subject area. In any case, the applicant is entitled to credit for only those subject areas satisfactorily completed. See the current revision of FAA Order 8900.2 for further information about retesting and allowable credit for subject areas satisfactorily completed.

Typical areas of unsatisfactory performance and grounds for disqualification include the following.

1. Any action or lack of action by the applicant that requires corrective intervention by the examiner for reasons of safety.
2. Failure to follow acceptable or approved maintenance procedures while performing projects.
3. Exceeding tolerances stated in the maintenance instructions.
4. Failure to recognize improper procedures.
5. The inability to perform to a return to service standard, where applicable.
6. Inadequate knowledge in any of the subject areas.

SECTION IV—POWERPLANT THEORY AND MAINTENANCE

A. RECIPROCATING ENGINES

REFERENCES: FAA-H-8083-32; AC 43.13-1B; 14 CFR part 43.

Objective. To determine that the applicant:

1. Exhibits knowledge in, as a minimum, two of the following elements—

    a. reciprocating engine theory of operation.
    b. basic radial engine design, components, and/or operation.
    c. firing order of a reciprocating engine.
    d. probable cause and removal of a hydraulic lock.
    e. valve adjustment on a radial engine.
    f. purpose of master and/or articulating rods.
    g. checks necessary to verify proper operation of a reciprocating engine.
    h. induction system leak indications.
    i. reciprocating engine maintenance procedures.
    j. procedures for inspecting various engine components during an overhaul.
    k. correct installation of piston rings and results of incorrectly installed or worn rings.
    l. purpose/function/operation of various reciprocating engine components, including, but not limited to, any of the following: crankshaft dynamic dampers, multiple springs for valves, piston rings, and reduction gearing.

2. Demonstrates skill to perform, as a minimum, one of the following elements—

    A1. Inspect a cylinder. (Level 2)
    A2. Remove and replace a stud. (Level 2)
    A3. Dimensionally inspect a crankshaft. (Level 2)
    A4. Install piston and/or knuckle pin(s). (Level 2)
    A5. Install cylinder assembly on an engine. (Level 3)
    A6. Identify the parts of a cylinder. (Level 2)
    A7. Identify the parts of a crankshaft. (Level 2)
    A8. Identify and inspect various types of bearings. (Level 2)
    A9. Replace packing seals in a push rod housing. (Level 2)
    A10. Check and/or rig cable and push-pull engine controls. (Level 3)
    A11. Adjust valve clearances. (Level 3)

A12. Inspect engine mounts. (Level 3)

A13. Demonstrate engine starting procedures. (Level 3)

A14. Operate an aircraft engine. (Level 3)

A15. Perform a cold cylinder check. (Level 3)

A16. Locate top dead-center position of a piston. (Level 3)

A17. Check cylinder compression with differential compression tester. (Level 3)

B. TURBINE ENGINES

REFERENCES: FAA-H-8083-32; AC 43.13-1B; 14 CFR part 43.

Objective. To determine that the applicant:

1. Exhibits knowledge in, as a minimum, two of the following elements—

    a. turbine engine theory of operation.
    b. checks necessary to verify proper operation.
    c. turbine engine troubleshooting procedures.
    d. procedures required after the installation of a turbine engine.
    e. causes for turbine engine performance loss.
    f. purpose/function/operation of various turbine engine components.
    g. turbine engine maintenance procedures.

2. Demonstrates skill to perform, as a minimum, one of the following elements—

    B1. Identify characteristics of different turbine compressors. (Level 2)
    B2. Identify types of turbine blades. (Level 2)
    B3. Identify major components of turbine engines. (Level 2)
    B4. Identify airflow direction and pressure changes in turbojet engines. (Level 2)
    B5. Remove and install a combustion case and liner. (Level 3)
    B6. Remove and install a fuel nozzle in a turbine engine. (Level 3)
    B7. Inspect combustion liners. (Level 3)
    B8. Measure turbine rotor blade clearance. (Level 3)
    B9. Locate procedures for the adjustment of a fuel control unit. (Level 1)
    B10. Perform turbine engine inlet guide vane and compressor blade inspection. (Level 3)
    B11. Locate the installation or removal procedures of a turbine engine. (Level 1)
    B12. Locate procedures for trimming a turbine engine. (Level 1)
    B13. Identify damaged turbine blades. (Level 3)
    B14. Identify causes for engine performance loss. (Level 2)
    B15. Remove and/or install a turbine rotor disk. (Level 3)
    B16. Identify damaged inlet nozzle guide vanes. (Level 3)
    B17. Inspect the first two stages of a turbine fan or compressor for foreign object damage. (Level 3)

NOTE: T. AUXILIARY POWER UNITS may be tested at the same time as AREA B. No further testing of auxiliary power units is required.

C. ENGINE INSPECTION

REFERENCES: FAA-H-8083-32; AC 43.13-1B; 14 CFR part 43.

Objective. To determine that the applicant:

1. Exhibits knowledge in, as a minimum, two of the following elements—

   a. the use of a type certificate data sheet (TCDS) to identify engine accessories.
   b. requirements for the installation or modification in accordance with a supplemental type certificate (STC).
   c. procedures for accomplishing a 100-hour inspection in accordance with the manufacturer's instruction.
   d. compliance with airworthiness directives.
   e. changes to an inspection program due to a change or modification required by airworthiness directive or service bulletin.
   f. determination of life limited parts.
   g. inspection required after a potentially damaging event, including but not limited to any of the following: sudden stoppage, over speed, or over temperature.

2. Demonstrates skill to perform, as a minimum, one of the following elements—

   C1. Inspect an engine for compliance with applicable ADs. (Level 3)
   C2. Identify an engine by type without reference material other than the data plate. (Level 2)
   C3. Determine engine conformity with engine specifications or type certificate data sheet. (Level 3)
   C4. Construct a checklist for a 100-hour inspection on an engine. (Level 2)
   C5. Perform a portion of the 100-hour inspection on an engine. (Level 3)
   C6. Check engine controls for freedom of operation. (Level 3)
   C7. Inspect an engine for fluid leaks after performance of maintenance. (Level 3)
   C9. Inspect aircraft engine accessories for conformity. (Level 3)
   C10. Inspect aircraft engine for service bulletin compliance. (Level 3)
   C11. Inspect aircraft turbine engine for records time left on any life limited parts. (Level 3)
   C12. Perform an over temperature inspection. (Level 3)
   C13. Perform an engine over torque inspection. (Level 3)
   C14. Perform an aircraft engine over speed inspection. (Level 3)
   C15. Determine conformity of installed spark plugs or igniters. (Level 3)
   C16. Determine if aircraft engine maintenance manual is current. (Level 2)

SECTION V—POWERPLANT SYSTEMS AND COMPONENTS

H. ENGINE INSTRUMENT SYSTEMS

REFERENCES: FAA-H-8083-32; AC 43.13-1B.

Objective. To determine that the applicant:

1. Exhibits knowledge in, as a minimum, two of the following elements—

   a. troubleshoot a fuel flow and/or low fuel pressure indicating system.
   b. the operation of a fuel flow indicating system and where it is connected to the engine.
   c. the operation of a temperature indicating system.
   d. the operation of a pressure indicating system.
   e. the operation of an revolutions per minute (RPM) indicating system.
   f. required checks to verify proper operation of a temperature indicating system.
   g. required checks to verify proper operation of a pressure indicating system.
   h. required checks to verify proper operation of an RPM indicating system.
   i. the operation of a manifold pressure gage and where it actually connects to an engine.

2. Demonstrates skill to perform, as a minimum, one of the following elements—

   H1. Remove, inspect, and/or install a fuel-flow transmitter. (Level 3)
   H2. Remove, inspect, and/or install fuel flow gage. (Level 3)
   H3. Identify various components installed on an engine. (Level 2)
   H4. Check fuel flow transmitter power supply. (Level 2)
   H5. Troubleshoot a fuel-flow system. (Level 3)
   H6. Inspect tachometer markings for accuracy. (Level 3)
   H7. Perform resistance measurements of thermocouple indication system. (Level 3)
   H8. Remove, inspect, and/or install turbine engine exhaust gas temperature (EGT) harness. (Level 3)
   H9. Troubleshoot a turbine engine pressure ratio (EPR) system. (Level 3)
   H10. Troubleshoot a tachometer system. (Level 3)

H11. Replace a cylinder head temperature thermocouple. (Level 3)

H12. Inspect EGT probes. (Level 2)

H13. Locate and inspect engine low fuel pressure warning system components. (Level 3)

H14. Check aircraft engine manifold pressure gage for proper operation. (Level 3)

H15. Inspect a leaking manifold pressure system. (Level 2)

H16. Repair a low oil pressure warning system. (Level 3)

H17. Troubleshoot an EGT indicating system. (Level 3)

I. ENGINE FIRE PROTECTION SYSTEMS

REFERENCES: FAA-H-8083-32; AC 43.13-1B.

Objective. To determine that the applicant:

1. Exhibits knowledge in, as a minimum, two of the following elements—

   a. checks to verify proper operation of an engine fire detection and/or extinguishing system.
   b. troubleshoots an engine fire detection and/or extinguishing system.
   c. inspection requirements for an engine fire extinguisher squib and safety practices/precautions.
   d. components and/or operation of an engine fire detection and/or extinguishing system.
   e. engine fire detection and/or extinguishing system maintenance procedures.

2. Demonstrates skill to perform, as a minimum, one of the following elements—

   I1. Identify fire detection sensing units. (Level 2)
   I2. Inspect fire detection continuous loop system. (Level 3)
   I3. Inspect fire detection thermal switch or thermocouple system. (Level 3)
   I4. Check and/or inspect a fire detection warning system. (Level 3)
   I5. Locate troubleshooting information for a fire detection system. (Level 1)
   I6. Inspect turbine engine fire detection system. (Level 3)
   I7. Inspect engine fire extinguisher system blowout plugs. (Level 3)
   I8. Inspect a turbine engine fire extinguisher agent container pressure. (Level 3)
   I9. Check fire extinguisher discharge circuit. (Level 3)
   I10. Troubleshoot a fire protection system. (Level 3)
   I11. Inspect fire extinguisher carbon dioxide bottle. (Level 3)
   I12. Repair fire detector heat sensing loop support clamps. (Level 3)
   I13. Inspect a fire extinguisher container discharge cartridge. (Level 3)
   I14. Inspect fire extinguisher system for hydrostatic test requirements. (Level 3)
   I15. Check flame detectors for operation. (Level 3)
   I16. Check operation of firewall shutoff valves. (Level 3)
   I17. Check operation of master caution press-to-test and troubleshoot faults. (Level 2)
   I18. Identify continuous-loop fire detection system components. (Level 2)

J. ENGINE ELECTRICAL SYSTEMS

REFERENCES: FAA-H-8083-32; AC 43.13-1B.

Objective. To determine that the applicant:

1. Exhibits knowledge in, as a minimum, two of the following elements—

    a. generator rating and performance data location.
    b. operation of a turbine engine starter-generator.
    c. the procedure for locating the correct electrical cable/wire size needed to fabricate a replacement cable/wire.
    d. installation practices for wires running close to exhaust stacks or heating ducts.
    e. operation of engine electrical system components.
    f. types of and/or components of direct current (DC) motors.
    g. inspection and/or replacement of starter-generator brushes.

2. Demonstrates skill to perform, as a minimum, one of the following elements—

    J1. Use publications to determine replacement part numbers. (Level 2)
    J2. Replace an engine-driven generator or alternator. (Level 3)
    J3. Service an engine-driven DC generator in accordance with manufacturer's instructions. (Level 3)
    J4. Parallel a dual-generator electrical system. (Level 3)
    J5. Inspect an engine-driven generator or alternator. (Level 3)
    J6. Troubleshoot a voltage regulator in an aircraft electrical generating system. (Level 2)
    J7. Repair an engine direct-drive electric starter. (Level 3)
    J8. Troubleshoot a direct-drive electric starter system. (Level 2)
    J9. Fabricate an electrical system cable. (Level 3)
    J10. Determine wire size for engine electrical system. (Level 2)
    J11. Repair a broken engine electrical system wire. (Level 3)
    J12. Replace a wire bundle lacing. (Level 3)
    J13. Identify an engine system electrical wiring schematic. (Level 2)
    J14. Fabricate a bonding jumper. (Level 3)
    J15. Inspect a turbine engine starter generator. (Level 3)
    J16. Fabricate solderless terminals. (Level 3)
    J17. Inspect engine electrical connectors. (Level 3)

K. LUBRICATION SYSTEMS

REFERENCES: FAA-H-8083-32; AC 43.13-1B.

Objective. To determine that the applicant:

1. Exhibits knowledge in, as a minimum, two of the following elements—

    a. differences between straight mineral oil, ashless-dispersant oil, and synthetic oil.
    b. types of oil used for different climates.
    c. functions of an engine oil.
    d. identification and selection of proper lubricants.
    e. servicing of the lubrication system.
    f. the reasons for changing engine lubricating oil at specified intervals.
    g. the purpose and operation of an oil/air separator.
    h. reasons for excessive oil consumption without evidence of oil leaks in a reciprocating and/or turbine aircraft engine.

2. Demonstrates skill to perform, as a minimum, one of the following elements—

    K1. Determine the correct type of oil for a specific engine. (Level 1)
    K2. Identify turbine engine oil filter bypass indicator. (Level 2)
    K3. Determine approved oils for different climatic temperatures. (Level 2)
    K4. Locate and describe procedures for changing turbine engine oil. (Level 1)
    K5. Inspect oil cooler and/or oil lines for leaks. (Level 3)
    K6. Inspect an oil filter or screen. (Level 3)
    K7. Check engine oil pressure. (Level 2)
    K8. Perform oil pressure adjustment. (Level 3)
    K9. Identify oil system components. (Level 2)
    K10. Replace an oil system component. (Level 3)
    K11. Identify oil system flow. (Level 2)
    K12. Service an oil tank. (Level 3)
    K13. Perform an engine pre-oil operation. (Level 3)
    K14. Troubleshoot an engine oil pressure malfunction. (Level 3)
    K15. Troubleshoot an engine oil temperature system. (Level 3)
    K16. Adjust oil Pressure. (Level 3)

L. IGNITION AND STARTING SYSTEMS

REFERENCE: FAA-H-8083-32; AC 43.13-1B.

Objective. To determine that the applicant:

1. Exhibits knowledge in, as a minimum, two of the following elements—

   a. troubleshooting a reciprocating and/or turbine engine ignition system.
   b. replacement of an exciter box and safety concerns if the box is damaged.
   c. troubleshooting a starter system.
   d. checking a starter system for proper operation.
   e. the operation of a pneumatic starting system.
   f. reasons for the starter dropout function of a starter generator or pneumatic starter.
   g. the purpose of a shear section in a starter output shaft.
   h. purpose of checking a p-lead for proper ground.
   i. inspection and servicing of an igniter and/or spark plug.
   j. magneto systems, components, and operation.
   k. function/operation of a magneto switch and p-lead circuit.
   l. high and low tension ignition systems.

2. Demonstrates skill to perform, as a minimum, one of the following elements—

   L1. Disassemble, identify components, and reassemble a magneto. (Level 3)
   L2. Inspect magneto breaker points. (Level 3)
   L3. Set internal timing of a magneto. (Level 3)
   L4. Test high-tension leads. (Level 3)
   L5. Remove and install an ignition harness. (Level 3)
   L6. Check a magneto on a test bench. (Level 3)
   L7. Check serviceability of condensers. (Level 3)
   L8. Check ignition coils. (Level 3)
   L9. Check ignition leads. (Level 3)
   L10. Troubleshoot ignition switch circuit. (Level 3)
   L11. Inspect and check gap of spark plugs. (Level 3)
   L12. Replace spark plugs. (Level 3)
   L13. Install and/or time a magneto on an engine. (Level 3)
   L14. Troubleshoot a turbine or reciprocating engine ignition system. (Level 3)
   L15. Replace turbine engine igniter plugs. (Level 3)
   L16. Troubleshoot turbine engine igniters. (Level 3)
   L17. Inspect turbine engine ignition system. (Level 3)
   L18. Fabricate an ignition lead. (Level 3)

M. FUEL METERING SYSTEMS

REFERENCE: FAA-H-8083-32; AC 43.13-1B.

Objective. To determine that the applicant:

1. Exhibits knowledge in, as a minimum, two of the following elements—

   a. troubleshooting an engine that indicates high exhaust gas temperature (EGT) for a particular engine pressure ratio (EPR).
   b. purpose of an acceleration check after a trim check.
   c. reasons an engine would require a trim check.
   d. purpose of the part power stop on some engines when accomplishing engine trim procedure.
   e. procedure required to adjust (trim) a fuel control unit (FCU).
   f. possible reasons for fuel running out of a carburetor throttle body.
   g. indications that would result if the mixture is improperly adjusted.
   h. procedure for checking idle mixture on a reciprocating engine.
   i. possible causes for poor engine acceleration, engine backfiring or missing when the throttle is advanced.
   j. types and operation of various fuel metering systems.
   k. fuel metering system components.

2. Demonstrates skill to perform, as a minimum, one of the following elements—

   M1. Remove, inspect, and install a turbine engine fuel nozzle. (Level 3)
   M2. Identify carburetor components. (Level 2)
   M3. Interpret diagram showing fuel and air flow through float-type and/or pressure type carburetor. (Level 2)
   M4. Remove and/or install a main metering jet in a carburetor. Level 3)
   M5. Service a carburetor fuel inlet screen. (Level 3)
   M6. Identify carburetor air-bleed system. (Level 2)
   M7. Identify the main discharge nozzle in a pressure carburetor. (Level 2)
   M8. Remove and/or install the accelerating pump in a float-type carburetor. (Level 3)
   M9. Check the float level on a float-type carburetor. (Level 3)
   M10. Remove and/or install the mixture control system in a float-type carburetor.(Level 3)

M11. Inspect float needle and/or seat in a float-type carburetor. (Level 3)

M12. Identify, remove, and/or install a float-type carburetor. (Level 3)

M13. Adjust idle speed and/or mixture. (Level 3)

M14. Inspect a turbine fuel control unit. (Level 3)

M15. Describe the conditions that may result in turbine engine RPM overspeed. (Level 2)

M16. Describe the conditions that may result in pressure carburetor engine with slow acceleration. (Level 2)

M17. Describe the conditions that may result in malfunctions in a pressure-injection carburetor fuel regulator unit. (Level 2)

M18. Replace a direct-injection fuel nozzle. (Level 3)

M19. Set or position fuel metering cockpit controls for engine start. (Level 2)

N. ENGINE FUEL SYSTEMS

REFERENCES: FAA-H-8083-32; AC 43.13-1B.

Objective. To determine that the applicant:

1. Exhibits knowledge in, as a minimum, two of the following
    elements—

    a. inspection requirements for an engine fuel system.
    b. checks of fuel systems to verify proper operation.
    c. troubleshooting an engine fuel system.
    d. procedure for inspection of an engine driven fuel pump for
        leaks and security.
    e. function and/or operation of one or more types of fuel
        pumps.
    f. function and/or operation of one or more types of fuel
        valves.
    g. function and/or operation of engine fuel filters.

2. Demonstrates skill to perform, as a minimum, one of the following
    elements—

    N1. Identify components of an engine fuel system. (Level 2)
    N2. Remove and/or install an engine-driven fuel pump.
             (Level 3)
    N3. Check a remotely operated fuel valve. (Level 3)
    N4. Rig a remotely operated fuel valve. (Level 3)
    N5. Inspect a main fuel filter assembly for leaks. (Level 3)
    N6. Check fuel boost pumps for correct pressure. (Level 2)
    N7. Remove and/or install a fuel boost pump. (Level 3)
    N8. Locate and identify a turbine engine fuel heater. (Level 2)
    N9. Check fuel pressure warning light function. (Level 2)
    N10. Adjust fuel pump fuel pressure. (Level 3)
    N11. Inspect engine fuel system fluid lines and/or
              components.(Level 3)
    N12. Troubleshoot abnormal fuel pressure. (Level 3)
    N13. Troubleshoot a turbine engine fuel heater system. (Level 3)
    N14. Remove, clean, and/or replace an engine fuel strainer.
              (Level 3)
    N15. Troubleshoot engine fuel pressure fluctuation. (Level 3)
    N16. Inspect fuel selector valve. (Level 3)
    N17. Determine correct fuel nozzle spray pattern. (Level 3)
    N18. Locate and identify fuel selector placards. (Level 2)

O. INDUCTION AND ENGINE AIRFLOW SYSTEMS

REFERENCES: FAA-H-8083-32; AC 43.13-1B.

Objective. To determine that the applicant:

1. Exhibits knowledge in, as a minimum, two of the following elements—

    a. inspection procedures for engine ice control systems and/or carburetor air intake and induction manifolds.
    b. operation of an alternate air valve, both automatic and manual heat systems.
    c. troubleshooting ice control systems.
    d. explain how a carburetor heat system operates and the procedure to verify proper operation.
    e. effect(s) on an aircraft engine if the carburetor heat control is improperly adjusted.
    f. causes and effects of induction system ice.
    g. function and operation of one or more types of supercharging systems and components.

2. Demonstrates skill to perform, as a minimum, one of the following elements—

    O1. Inspect a carburetor preheat system. (Level 2)
    O2. Check a carburetor heater box shutter for full travel. (Level 2)
    O3. Check carburetor heat. (Level 3)
    O4. Identify probable location of induction ice. (Level 2)
    O5. Identify turbine engine air intake ice protected areas. (Level 2)
    O6. Service an induction air filter. (Level 3)
    O7. Inspect a turbocharger for exhaust leaks and security. (Level 2)
    O8. Check a turbocharger for operation. (Level 3)
    O9. Inspect an induction system for obstruction. (Level 3)
    O10. Inspect an air intake manifold for leaks. (Level 3)
    O11. Troubleshoot engine that idles poorly. (Level 2)
    O12. Troubleshoot engine that fails to start. (Level 2)
    O13. Identify components of a turbocharger induction system. (Level 2)
    O14. Troubleshoot a carburetor heat system. (Level 2)
    O15. Troubleshoot turbine engine air inlet ice protection system. (Level 2)
    O16. Identify turboprop engine ice and rain protection system components. (Level 2)
    O17. Remove, inspect, and/or install a turbocharger. (Level 3)
    O18. Inspect a carburetor air inlet duct attachment. (Level 2)

P. ENGINE COOLING SYSTEMS

REFERENCES: FAA-H-8083-32; AC 43.13-1B.

Objective. To determine that the applicant:

1. Exhibits knowledge in, as a minimum, two of the following elements—

   a. required inspection on an engine cooling system.
   b. operation of cowl flaps, and how cooling is accomplished.
   c. how turbine engine cooling is accomplished.
   d. cooling of engine bearings and other parts on turbine engines.
   e. the importance of proper engine baffle and seal installation.
   f. the operation of a heat exchanger.
   g. the function and operation of an augmentor cooling system.
   h. rotorcraft engine cooling systems.

2. Demonstrates skill to perform, as a minimum, one of the following elements—

   P1. Repair cylinder head baffle. (Level 3)
   P2. Inspect cylinder head baffle plates. (Level 2)
   P3. Check cowl flap travel. (Level 3)
   P4. Inspect cylinder cooling fins. (Level 2)
   P5. Repair cylinder cooling fin. (Level 3)
   P6. Identify location of turbine engine insulation blankets. (Level 2)
   P7. Identify turbine engine cooling air flow. (Level 2)
   P8. Troubleshoot a cowl flap system. (Level 3)
   P9. Troubleshoot an engine cooling system. (Level 3)
   P10. Identify exhaust augmentor cooled engine components. (Level 2)
   P11. Repair turbine engine insulation blankets. (Level 3)
   P12. Identify rotorcraft engine cooling components. (Level 2)
   P13. Troubleshoot rotorcraft engine cooling system. (Level 3)
   P14. Inspect rotorcraft engine cooling system. (Level 3)
   P15. Inspect engine exhaust augmentor cooling system. (Level 3)

Q. ENGINE EXHAUST AND REVERSER SYSTEMS

REFERENCES: FAA-H-8083-32; AC 43.13-1B.

Objective. To determine that the applicant:

1. Exhibits knowledge in, as a minimum, two of the following elements—

    a. exhaust leak indications and/or methods of detection.
    b. thrust reverser system operation and components.
    c. differences between a cascade and a mechanical blockage door thrust reverser.
    d. hazards of exhaust system failure.
    e. effects of using improper materials to mark on exhaust system components.
    f. function and operation of various exhaust system components.

2. Demonstrates skill to perform, as a minimum, one of the following elements—

    Q1. Identify the type of exhaust system on a particular aircraft. (Level 2)
    Q2. Inspect exhaust system components. (Level 2)
    Q3. Repair exhaust system components. (Level 3)
    Q4. Clean exhaust system components. (Level 2)
    Q5. Inspect reciprocating engine exhaust system. (Level 3)
    Q6. Inspect exhaust system internal baffles or diffusers. (Level 3)
    Q7. Remove and install exhaust ducts. (Level 3)
    Q8. Inspect exhaust heat exchanger. (Level 3)
    Q9. Remove and install a heat exchanger collector tube. (Level 3)
    Q10. Perform a heat exchanger collector tube leak test. (Level 3)
    Q11. Inspect a turbine engine exhaust nozzle. (Level 3)
    Q12. Check turbine thrust reverser system. (Level 3)
    Q13. Troubleshoot a thrust reverser system. (Level 2)
    Q14. Troubleshoot exhaust muffler heat exchanger. (Level 2)
    Q15. Repair exhaust system leak. (Level 3)
    Q16. Locate procedures for performing exhaust system leak checks. (Level 2)

R. PROPELLERS

REFERENCES: FAA-H-8083-32; AC 43.13-1B.

Objective. To determine that the applicant:

1. Exhibits knowledge in, as a minimum, two of the following elements—

    a. propeller theory of operation.
    b. checks necessary to verify proper operation of propeller systems.
    c. procedures for proper application of propeller lubricants.
    d. installation or removal of a propeller.
    e. measurement of blade angle with a propeller protractor.
    f. repairs classified as major repairs on an aluminum propeller.
    g. reference data for reducing the diameter of a type certificated propeller.
    h. operation of propeller system component(s).
    i. propeller governor components and operation.
    j. theory and operation of various types of constant speed propellers.
    k. function and operation of propeller synchronizing systems.
    l. function and operation of propeller ice control systems.

2. Determine what minor propeller alterations are acceptable using the appropriate type certificate data sheet. (Level 2) and a minimum of at least one of the following—

    R1. Perform propeller lubrication. (Level 3)
    R2. Locate the procedures for balancing a fixed-pitch propeller. (Level 1)
    R3. Remove, inspect, and/or install a propeller governor. (Level 3)
    R4. Remove and/or install a propeller. (Level 3)
    R5. Check track of a propeller. (Level 3)
    R6. Adjust a propeller governor. (Level 3)
    R7. Determine propeller blade pitch angle. (Level 3)
    R8. Determine propeller critical range of operation. (Level 2)
    R9. Describe the operation of a propeller. (Level 2)
    R10. Inspect a wooden propeller metal tipping. (Level 3)
    R11. Check propeller blade feather angle. (Level 3)
    R12. Repair metal propeller leading edges, trailing edges or tips that have nicks, scratches, and cuts. (Level 3)
    R13. Clean an aluminum alloy propeller. (Level 2)
    R14. Inspect a turboprop propeller system. (Level 3)
    R15. Perform a 100-hour inspection on a propeller. (Level 3)
    R16. Troubleshoot a turboprop propeller system. (Level 3)
    R17. Repair anti-icing or de-icing system on a propeller. (Level 2)

S. TURBINE POWERED AUXILIARY POWER UNITS

REFERENCE: FAA-H-8083-32; AC 43.13-1B.

Objective. To determine that the applicant:

1. Exhibits knowledge in, as a minimum, two of the following elements—

   a. inspection to ensure proper operation of turbine driven auxiliary power unit.
   b. replacement procedure for an igniter plug.
   c. servicing an auxiliary power unit.
   d. troubleshooting an auxiliary power unit.
   e. function and operation of auxiliary power unit(s).

NOTE: Subject area S, AUXILIARY POWER UNITS, may be tested at the same time as AREA B, TURBINE ENGINES. No further testing of auxiliary power units is required.